DATE DUE

Volunteerism and Older Adults

Choices and Challenges:
An Older Adult Reference Series
Elizabeth Vierck, Series Editor

Housing Options and Services for Older Adults,
Ann E. Gillespie and Katrinka Smith Sloan

Mental Health Problems and Older Adults,
Gregory A. Hinrichsen

Older Workers, Sara E. Rix

Paying for Health Care after Age 65,
Elizabeth Vierck

Volunteerism and Older Adults, Mary K. Kouri

Forthcoming

Legal Issues and Older Adults,
Linda Josephson Millman and Sallie Birket Chafer

Travel and Older Adults, Allison St. Claire

Volunteerism and Older Adults

Mary K. Kouri

Choices and Challenges: An Older Adult Reference Series
Elizabeth Vierck, Series Editor

ABC-CLIO

Santa Barbara, California
Oxford, England

Cover Design/Graphein

Library of Congress Cataloging-in-Publication Data
Kouri, Mary K., 1943–
     Volunteerism and older adults / Mary K. Kouri.
        p.   cm.—(Choices and challenges)
     Includes bibliographical references and index.
     1. Voluntarism—United States.   2. Aged volunteers—United States.
     I. Title.   II. Series.
     HN90.V64K68   1990   361.3'7—dc20   90-43056

ISBN 0-87436-562-7 (alk. paper)

97 96 95 94 93 92 91 90   10 9 8 7 6 5 4 3 2 1

ABC-CLIO, Inc.
130 Cremona Drive, P.O. Box 1911
Santa Barbara, California 93116-1911

Clio Press Ltd.
55 St. Thomas' Street
Oxford, OX1 1JG, England

This book is Smyth-sewn and printed on acid-free paper ∞.
Manufactured in the United States of America

Contents

Preface

It is becoming a truism that the fastest-growing segment of the U.S. population is adults aged 65 and older. People in the latter stages of life face challenges, problems, and opportunities that are very different from those of younger adults. Choices and Challenges is a series of reference books designed to provide older adults with information and resources uniquely suited to their needs and interests. This volume addresses a topic of increasing interest to retired adults: volunteerism.

People volunteer for a wide range of reasons, from a desire to serve others to a need to acquire skills that can lead to paid employment, and to personal satisfaction and enjoyment. Whatever the reasons, millions of older adults each year seek out volunteer opportunities in a multitude of fields. The purpose of this book is to provide older adults interested in volunteering with guidance in finding the work that best suits their interests, skills, and expectations. Directors of volunteer programs and professionals who work with older adults, such as program directors and counselors in senior residences and community centers, will also find it useful.

The book is divided into two parts of several chapters each and contains an index for easy reference. Readers may read Part One straight through and then consult Part Two for further resources on specific topics, browse through either section, or use the index to locate specific information.

Part One is a narrative section that provides background information and guidance for exploring the many types of volunteer opportunities available. The Introduction places volunteerism in its historical and social context. It then explores the concept of older adults as a vast and largely untapped resource for meeting social needs both within and outside of the monetized economy. Chapter 1 provides an overview of volunteerism.

It includes the many areas where volunteers serve, examples of how people integrate volunteerism into their daily lives, and statistical information on the topic. Chapter 2, "Finding Volunteer Opportunities," explains how to conduct a self-assessment to identify one's interests, preferred skills, and desired rewards. It then describes how to find the volunteer work that best satisfies both these desires and the volunteer's personal circumstances. Chapter 3 provides useful suggestions for volunteer directors and others who work with older volunteers.

Part Two is a resource guide for the potential volunteer as well as the volunteer manager seeking in-depth information on the topics covered in Part One. Chapter 4 is an annotated directory of organizations, associations, government agencies, and self-help groups. Groups are listed alphabetically for easy reference. Chapter 5 is an annotated bibliography of printed reference materials, including books, directories, periodicals, newsletters, manuals, and pamphlets, as well as journal, magazine, and newspaper articles. The references are grouped according to type and listed alphabetically by author within each group. Chapter 6 is an annotated directory of nonprint references, including databases, nonprint media, and audiovisual materials. These also are grouped by type and then listed alphabetically by title within each group.

Acknowledgments

This project has been the mix of joy and dejection that most authors encounter when they set out to write a book. One of the joys during these months was working with people who contributed so much to this task. My editors, Laurie Brock and Betsy Vierck, are two of the most competent and helpful associates I could imagine. Their suggestions and insights improved every chapter. I particularly appreciated their kindness and patience as I fumbled toward an understanding of how to write a reference book. My friend and professional colleague Yancey Stockwell was always supportive and many times helped me regain my sense of humor when my seriousness got out of proportion. The reference librarians at the Denver Public Library and Arapahoe County Christensen Library are cheerful wizards who could produce, in moments, information that I thought I would be lucky to have within days. My thanks to all the agencies and publishers who filled my mailbox with hundreds of pounds of brochures, samples, and review copies that eventually found their way into this book. To the volunteer directors and the volunteers who patiently answered my questions and gave permission to print their ideas—thank you. Their wisdom and stories bring the human touch to these pages. Thanks to my family and friends for their enthusiasm and encouragement.

Volunteerism
and
Older Adults

Introduction

> What we get makes a living. What we give makes a life.
>
> —Winston Churchill

Adults over 65 represent the fastest-growing segment of the U.S. population, yet they lack a well-defined societal role. For many older Americans, volunteerism offers a pathway for channeling energy, knowledge, and productivity back into the mainstream of society. This book explores the many opportunities offered by volunteerism and offers a guide both for older adults who are considering volunteer work and for professionals who work with older volunteers.

Volunteerism: An Enduring American Tradition

On a visit to the United States in 1831, French statesman and philosopher Alexis de Tocqueville noted the conspicuous presence of volunteerism. "Americans of all ages, all conditions, and all dispositions constantly form associations,"[1] he wrote. "I have often admired the extreme skill with which the inhabitants of the United States succeed in proposing a common object for the exertions of a great many men and inducing them voluntarily to pursue it."[2]

That tradition of volunteerism is stronger than ever today, and a new dimension has been added. The United States of Tocqueville's time was a frontier nation with abundant and seemingly inexhaustible natural resources and a population whose median age was only 17. In 1990 the median age has nearly doubled to 33, and both natural and economic resources seem severely limited. Yet one natural resource is growing rapidly—the knowledge, skills, and energy possessed by an expanding population of

3

older adults. Volunteerism is a channel through which this growing resource can serve many needs in today's society.

The Young-Old

Clean living conditions, safe workplaces, and healthy life-styles are enabling ever larger numbers of people to achieve middle age and to live well beyond it. Prior to the creation of Social Security in 1935, few Americans planned to retire. "Most workers retired only when ill. . . . The years after retirement were few, and the choices of life-style were limited by poor health."[3] In 1935, only 6 percent of the population was 65 or older. By contrast:

- Today one in four U.S. citizens is age 50 or older. Twelve percent of the population is age 65 or over.

- At age 50, people can expect to live an average of 28 more years; 65 year-olds have an average life expectancy of almost 17 more years.

- Of the 29.8 million people aged 65 or older, 88 percent (26.6 million) are retired.

- The average American now spends one-quarter of his or her adult life in retirement.[4]

The large number of adults in this previously uncommon stage of life led gerontologist Bernice Neugarten to coin the term "young-old"—that period when an individual has passed middle age yet continues to enjoy good health and to fully participate in family and community affairs.[5] Young-old refers to a set of health and social characteristics rather than chronological age. In this frame of reference, a young-old person might be 57 or 83 years old.

Neugarten uses the term "old-old" for the life stage marked by frailty and limited capacity to engage independently in the activities of daily life. These limitations usually force individuals to scale down or modify their participation in family or community life. Neugarten emphasized the unreliability of chronological age as a predictor of vitality. Even in the over-85 age group, she found that one-third report no health-related problems, one-third report some limitations, and one-third cannot carry out daily activities.[6]

A large number of older adults enjoy the gifts of health, comfortable finances, education, and discretionary time. Social Security, pensions, and personal savings plans enable the majority of retired adults to live comfortably; the median income of families where the head of household is age 65 or over is approximately $20,000. Today's older adults are also better educated, with 12 median years of schooling compared with 8.7 years in 1970. And they are still learning, often for the sheer pleasure of it. Harry Moody reported that the number of people over age 65 who participate in adult-education courses is growing at the rate of 30 percent every three years.[7] Other studies suggest that adults are more likely to be involved in learning projects, whether formal or self-directed, after age 65 than between the ages of 55 and 64.

Retirement Is a Burden to Some

Although many retired people lead full lives rich with activities, friends, and family relationships, others find that retirement is a barrier to the productivity, participation, and status they enjoyed as members of the paid work force. They may even feel, as did playwright Kenneth Bernard, that retirement is "an immediate, and usually irrevocable step into second-class citizenship."[8] Retirement and age-discrimination specialist Malcolm Morrison noted that individuals who find meaning in their lives through involvement with work, family, and community are vulnerable to the "assumption that their further productivity—in the broad sense—will be neither required nor expected."[9]

From a societal point of view, the retired population represents an increasing burden rather than an asset. Diminishing numbers of young and middle-aged workers are being forced to shoulder a larger share of the taxes required to support the long-lived retirees. Phillip Longman, of Americans for Generational Equity, noted that the baby-boom generation, born between 1946 and 1964, is the first in U.S. history to be larger than the one following it.[10] In 1980, 25 percent of the work force were young people in the 16 to 24 age group.[11] By 1995, this up-and-coming group will decline to 16 percent of the work force. These figures are particularly dramatic when described in terms of workers available to pay for Social Security benefits. In 1935 there were 150 workers for each beneficiary. The ratio is currently 3.4 workers per beneficiary, which will fall to two workers per beneficiary as the baby boomers begin turning 65 in the year 2010. The "baby bust" generation will be at a double disadvantage. It will be supporting retirement benefits for a group larger than itself, while bearing the burden of the present national debt.

Given these circumstances, the institution of public policies that will enable the continued productivity of older adults is more than a humanitarian issue. It is an economic imperative. The skills, knowledge, and energy of millions of retired adults represent a largely unmined resource for meeting a vast assortment of societal needs through both paid and volunteer contributions. At the same time, volunteerism offers older adults the opportunity to remain participating, productive members of the society.

A Broader Vision of Productivity

In his proposal for new policies on aging, Harry Moody asks, "Is a society of jobholders really an adequate vision of an aging society or of the good society?"[12] He argues instead for a broader definition of productivity and growth that would create resources by enlarging and fully using human capabilities. This new vision includes "nonmonetized"[13] as well as traditional monetized forms of contribution. In nonmonetized transactions, resources such as time, services, or material goods are the means of exchange rather than money. Paid jobs represent monetized productivity, and volunteer jobs represent nonmonetized productivity. Both are necessary to a realistic vision of productivity for elder citizens in the coming decades. The needs of individuals in all age groups will be better served by such a vision.

Productivity through Employment

In the near future, people's needs for paid jobs will likely continue well beyond the current median age of retirement at 61, because of such factors as reduced Social Security benefits, lower real earning power, inflation, heavy tax burdens, and delayed childbearing. Couples who become parents in their thirties and forties are apt to need jobs in their fifties and sixties to pay for their children's college tuition. At the same time, worker shortages could make it necessary for employers to hire or retain workers who are well into their sixties or even seventies, as demonstrated by the fast-food industry's current efforts to recruit older workers.

For many people, paid employment remains an essential link to self-esteem and productivity. They see it as demeaning to ask older adults to contribute their skills and knowledge, honed over many years, without monetary compensation. "It lowers the dignity of your work if you are doing the same thing as a younger person and not getting paid for it," said a proponent of this view.

Productivity through Volunteerism

Volunteerism can claim equal status with paid work as a legitimate form of productivity for several reasons:

1. Volunteerism offers an avenue for learning new skills or adapting existing ones for use in paid jobs.

    For example, Priscilla Hawthorne combined volunteer work and formal schooling to forge a new career. She enrolled in a horticulture program at a community college; at the same time she served two volunteer internships, one at a city botanical garden and the other in the greenhouse of a community hospital. At age 69, the former social worker took a job at a commercial nursery. Later, she earned a master gardener's certificate through the county extension. She "paid" for her training by staffing the community garden hotline at the county extension office.

    Similarly, Sara Coleman, a 62-year-old real estate broker, wanted to leave the competitive world of real estate, but was not financially or emotionally ready to retire. Following a lifelong fascination with the written word, she became a library volunteer, with the goal of eventually getting paid for "working with books."

Within a year she was offered a job in the library, which she intends to hold at least through her sixties.

2. Volunteerism provides support for institutions and causes that have "low potential for profit and high potential for the national good."[14]

Danzig and Szanton named some of these: education, health care, child care, environmental preservation, criminal justice, and civic institutions. They estimated the need for service and productive activity in these areas to be the equivalent of 3.5 million jobs. Each area poses complex problems whose management requires the mixture of skills and experience, judgment and wisdom that many older adults have accumulated through decades of living.

Ted Cobb, for example, chose to tackle the problem of high-school dropouts. The retired president of a temporary-help service spearheaded a project by the Denver Rotary Club to encourage high-school graduation among the city's teenagers. His proposal outlined choices for Rotary members' individual and company participation: mentoring, part-time jobs contingent on school attendance, programs to encourage dropouts to pass the high-school equivalency exam (GED), and support of other community programs aimed toward strengthening public education. Cobb used the respect he had earned after working many years in the business community to focus his colleagues' attention on the need to improve graduation rates; thus, he created positive changes in both individual lives and in his community.

3. Volunteerism serves a personal need to "give back" to the world.

As they enter the latter part of their lives, many people feel an obligation to leave a legacy in appreciation for gifts received over a lifetime. They experience a sense of completion when they put something back into the human treasury.

For Helen and Bruce Fickel, "Volunteering is our way of paying the rent for the space we take on the earth." Part of their legacy of appreciation was their effort to preserve the past of their hometown of Berthoud, Colorado. They helped renovate historic spots and saved many artifacts of the Rocky Mountain community's mining days.

Omar Gaskin, retired postal carrier, also repaid a debt of gratitude through volunteer work. As a young man, he had been frustrated by his inability to help his sister care for her son, who was born with a birth defect and lived only a few years. The sister lived hundreds of miles away, and Gaskin's obligations to his own wife and children took all of his time and resources. Through the years, however, he remembered his gratitude to the volunteers who gave his sister the support and respite he was unable to provide. After retiring, he repaid the debt by working 20 hours or more each week at a Volunteers of America food bank. "It's my way of saying 'Thanks,' " he explained.

The Many Faces of Volunteerism

Volunteer work still thrives in its traditional forms of service to the poor, the needy, and the sick. Beyond these well-known forms, however, are new kinds of volunteer service that touch other dimensions of individual lives and address other needs of modern society. The following examples describe some activities in which giving is its own reward. Others are examples of non-monetized exchanges of service for other services or goods. All the examples illustrate the value of innovative volunteer activity in the lives of individuals and their communities.

Volunteerism To Strengthen Families and Neighborhoods

When families live in close proximity, older members can share responsibilities as well as receive support from younger members. For example, an older relative can provide cooking or child care for working parents. As extended family members move away from each other to follow educational and employment opportunities, however, the flow of give-and-take between generations diminishes.

The loss of such contacts creates gaps in many lives. Young and middle-aged adults lose the vision of their own future that older adults provide implicitly by their presence and explicitly through sharing their experience of the journey through the life cycle. Children have no firsthand view of different styles of aging or access to information about the "old days." They also have limited opportunities for unconditional acceptance by adults who can appreciate the wonders of childhood with freedom from the duties of parenthood.

In the same way, older people lose a rich dimension of life when they are isolated from contact with younger persons. They miss out on the enlivening contact with youthful energy, and an avenue of involvement with the future that will unfold after they complete their own lives.

Volunteerism provides a means for reestablishing this contact between generations and within neighborhoods, and for providing support to families and individuals. For example, KanWork in Wichita, Kansas, helps families move from welfare dependency to financial independence. It recruits volunteers, particularly older adults, to serve as family mentors. The mentors agree to spend two hours each week for at least six months giving support and guidance to individuals and their families as they move toward independence.

In Boulder, Colorado, trained volunteers offer mediation services. They help settle disputes involving parents and their teen-aged children, landlords and tenants, neighbors, and community groups. Disputed issues can include withholding of security deposits, barking dogs, conflicts over shared driveways, or community zoning changes. Judy Dixon, a four-year volunteer mediator, says, "It's satisfying to be able to help people solve their own disputes without going to court. Often they save thousands of dollars. Sometimes they are able to settle conflicts that have already cost thousands of dollars. Our settlement rate is 90 percent."

"Don't Move, Improve" is the motto of the Council of Community Clubs that Ferdia Harris founded in South Central Los

Angeles, California. Area residents organized 35 block clubs whose members keep their neighborhoods clean, communicate with city government, refer residents to community services, and maintain cooperative relationships with local businesses.

Many handicapped and frail elderly are in nursing homes because the lack of in-home assistance for them and their families leaves no other alternative.

Although community care is preferable to institutional care, it requires more time and energy than many families can give. Volunteer programs such as Meals-on-Wheels, active in many cities throughout the country, make it possible for older people to remain in their own homes and communities.

Volunteerism in City Government

In many parts of the nation, budgets at all levels of government are suffering from eroded tax bases. The resulting service reduction leaves many individuals and communities without services that could make their lives more manageable. Volunteers provide a means for filling these gaps.

In city governments, especially, volunteers are becoming a strong presence, participating in such wide-ranging activities as fighting fires, doing clerical work, training video-equipment operators, and designing computer programs. Increasingly, they assist with public safety and law enforcement, as illustrated by the examples below. In all of these areas, volunteers allow the city to do more with available funds. According to a survey by University of Idaho professor Sidney Duncombe,[15] both volunteers and their supervisors agree on this point. He reported that 98 percent of the supervisors believed the benefits of using volunteers outweighed the costs.

"In a department our size and a city our size," said Police Chief Richard Ruonala of Goose Creek, South Carolina, "we couldn't survive without this volunteer help."[16] Volunteers in this Charleston suburb operate a computer calling system that makes check-in calls to older citizens. If a person does not answer the call or indicates a need for assistance, the system sets into motion a series of phone and personal contacts.

In Detroit, Michigan, volunteers staff police ministations in storefront offices and low-income housing projects. They take calls, record major crimes on a map, keep the books, and do other office chores. In other cities, older volunteers assist elderly crime victims with referrals to community-service agencies. They log crime reports, enter data on computers, and make preliminary studies of crime patterns and trends before turning them over to police officers for in-depth study.

George Sunderland, a former policeman, heads the American Association of Retired Persons' (AARP) Criminal Justice Section. He observed that AARP has more requests than it can handle from police departments that want to be trained to work with volunteers. When the program started 17 years ago, Sunderland said, "You couldn't mention the subject, because you'd be laughed out of the room."[17]

Volunteerism as "Currency" in the Community Marketplace

In the nonmonetized economy, volunteer work is a form of currency to be exchanged for goods or services. Barter is a familiar example: trading something one has for something one needs or wants, such as doing a neighbor's laundry in exchange for transportation. Organized bartering programs are springing up throughout the country. The following examples offer a glimpse at their potential for developing self-reliance and productivity in community and individual lives.

Service banks enable people to earn and store credits for later use. The concept is described by social-work professor Catherine Goodman: "A deposit represents a payment of labor, which provides entitlement for withdrawal, from the bank, of similar services by the depositor."[18] A model service bank is the Service Credit Volunteer System in Washington, D.C. It is open to anyone over age 65 regardless of income. Participants perform chores for others and receive credits that are banked in a computerized bookkeeping system. When they need services, they can draw upon their accumulated credits. Depositors may also transfer credits they earn to the account of a friend or relative.[19]

The SHARE-USA project, an innovative combination of volunteerism and barter, stretches the power of limited cash. Once a month participants may buy a bag of fresh and packaged food. The price is a combination of cash and volunteer service. The cash price is approximately one-third of the food's retail value and it can be paid in currency or food stamps. Each buyer performs two hours of volunteer service with either the SHARE program or a service agency in the community. People of all ages and income levels are welcome to participate. The program is spreading throughout the United States. Each state chapter uses the state's name, for example, SHARE-California. For further information on this project, refer to the description of SHARE-USA in Chapter 4.

Mutual Self-Help

Mutual self-help is another form of nonmonetized productivity that enhances interdependence and self-reliance in communities and among individuals. It eases the pinch of money shortages or scarce services. "Many of the vital needs of the elderly—in health, crime prevention, nutrition, and long-term care—can be met by systematic programs of mutual self-help."[20] One of the hallmarks of such groups is their informality. They are run by members rather than professionals. The members give and receive help as needed.

Self-help groups and projects can center around any number of issues such as health, drug abuse, weight control, grandparents' rights, crime prevention, or food production. As an example, Moody described the activities of Court Watch, a group of older citizens in suburban New York City. Individual members contacted age-mates who had been crime victims and offered them personal support. Group members also regularly appeared at trials to support stiff sentences for criminals who victimize the elderly.

In Cheyenne, Wyoming, citizens cooperated in running a communal solar greenhouse to produce their own food. The elderly worked along with children, the handicapped, juvenile offenders, and others from the community to contribute physical energy, gardening know-how, engineering knowledge, food-storage techniques, recipes, and stories of Wyoming history.

According to Moody, self-help offers three benefits for older adults. First, it meaningfully involves their nonmonetized productive capacities. Second, it builds new community institutions that help individuals overcome social isolation. Finally, it engages older adults in contributing to the social good while enhancing their own well-being.[21] Bruce Stokes, a global-trends researcher at the Worldwatch Institute wrote, "Through self-help activities, the psychology of dependence can be replaced by a growing sense of self-reliance."[22] For further information on self-help groups, refer to the description of the Self-Help Clearinghouse in Chapter 4.

Future Trends in Volunteerism

It is said that in 1899 the U.S. Patent Office chief recommended that the office be closed down because it was not needed anymore. Everything important had already been invented. Just as the patent office saw some revolutionary inventions after 1899, volunteerism will see many inventions in the 1990s. Here is a glimpse at a few of the possibilities.

Vouchers for Volunteer Service in Government

The time-tested concept of vouchers or coupons could have new applications in nonmonetized forms of productivity. Citizens could earn vouchers through service in government agencies. In turn, the vouchers could be used to offset tax payments or to obtain government-provided goods and services.

For instance, a person who works as an aide in an after-school program at the local elementary school might use his voucher to reduce property taxes. Another citizen might teach fire safety to schools and businesses while earning vouchers redeemable for similar tax reductions.

Vouchers earned for service in government agencies could have open-ended redemption value as well as the specific uses suggested above. For example, citizens could do volunteer jobs in agencies and earn units of service from government agencies of their choice. They could exchange their vouchers for such items as tickets to municipal opera performances or tuition at a community college where they could study new skills to use in paid jobs.

Volunteerism in Business

The trend of business cooperation in community life is growing. The following are possibilities for furthering corporate citizenship through voluntary service. A utility company might train volunteers to conduct energy audits or to teach energy conservation measures. The volunteers could then trade their services for reductions on their utility bills. A grocery store might cooperate with volunteers who shop for or assist persons who are unable to shop independently. In return, the volunteers could receive discounts on their own food purchases.

Service Insurance

Goodman suggested a highly sophisticated form of service exchange. She proposed a system whereby volunteers would work a predetermined number of hours and, therefore, become eligible to receive services when they needed them. Goodman stressed that her proposal is based on an insurance model, so claims for service would be evaluated against preset criteria before they would be approved. Because participants would be insuring themselves against a time when they would need service, they would not all collect an equal share of service.[23]

Multipurpose Mutual Self-Help Networks

Gaps in the care of the frail elderly are only partially filled by professional and volunteer service programs. Many who need the help cannot afford to pay for it. A 1988 report of the Commonwealth Fund Commission said, "The majority of poor elderly people with serious chronic health problems live alone."[24] Self-help groups could fill some of the needs for companionship, for assistance in shopping, cooking, cleaning, and transportation, as well as emotional support through the pain of illness and loss.

Productive Activity for Frail and Disabled Elders

Physical and mental limitations do not signify total incapacity for most people. "In every situation, for every person, there is a realm of freedom and a realm of constraint," said Allen Wheelis.[25] Productive activity is possible using those capabilities that are not affected by illness or disability, and with technology the realm of freedom can be expanded even further. The telephone has done so for decades. Now computers, fax machines, and video equipment serve as partners to human ingenuity.

For example, nursing-home residents could act as security monitors for shopping malls and buildings, using bedside television screens that transmit the activity captured by security cameras. At the sight of potential problems, residents would press buzzers to alert staff on the premises.

In the ways described here, and in many still to be invented, volunteerism is an essential part of a new vision of productivity and fulfillment for older adults. It holds rich possibilities for personal growth and participation in the give-and-take of community life.

Notes

1. Alexis de Tocqueville, "Of the Use Which the Americans Make of Public Associations in Civil Life," in *America's Voluntary Spirit: A Book of Readings,* ed. Brian O'Connell (New York: The Foundation Center, 1983), 53.
2. Ibid., 54.
3. Mary K. Kouri, "From Retirement to Re-Engagement: Young Elders Forge New Futures," *Futurist* 28 (June 1984): 35.
4. Matilda White Riley and John W. Riley, Jr., "Longevity and Social Structure: The Potential of the Added Years," in *Our Aging Society: Paradox and Promise,* ed. Alan Pifer and Lydia Bronte (New York: W. W. Norton, 1986), 59.
5. Bernice L. Neugarten, "Age Groups in American Society and the Rise of the Young-Old," *Annals of the American Academy of Political and Social Sciences* 415 (September 1974): 187.
6. Bernice L. Neugarten and Dail A. Neugarten, "Changing Meanings of Age in the Aging Society," in *Our Aging Society,* ed. Pifer and Bronte, 35.
7. Harry R. Moody, *The Abundance of Life: Human Development Policies for an Aging Society* (New York: Columbia University Press, 1988), 192.
8. Kenneth Bernard, "The First Step to the Cemetery," *Newsweek,* 22 February 1982, 15.
9. Malcolm H. Morrison, "Work and Retirement in an Older Society," in *Our Aging Society,* ed. Pifer and Bronte, 343.
10. Phillip Longman, "Age Wars: The Coming Battle between Young and Old," *Futurist* 20 (January/February 1986): 8.
11. Phillip Longman, "The Challenge of an Aging Society," *Futurist* 22 (September/October 1988): 34.
12. Moody, *Abundance of Life,* 39.
13. Ibid.
14. Richard Danzig and Peter Szanton, *National Service: What Would It Mean?* (Lexington, MA: Lexington Books, D. C. Heath & Co., 1986): 41.
15. Sydney Duncombe, "Volunteers in City Government," *National Civic Review* 75 (September/October 1986): 293.
16. Ordway P. Burden, "Volunteers: The Wave of the Future?" *Police Chief* 55 (July 1988): 25.
17. Ibid., 29.
18. Catherine Chase Goodman, "Helper Bank: A Reciprocal Services Program for Older Adults," *Social Work* 29 (July/August 1984): 397.
19. For further information on the operation of, and a debate on the pros and cons of service banks, review the U.S. Senate hearing on the subject: Committee on Labor and

Human Resources, Subcommittee on Aging. *Volunteer Service Promotion Act of 1987.* 100th Cong., 1st sess., 12 November 1987.
20. Moody, 169.
21. Ibid., 176.
22. Bruce Stokes, "Helping Ourselves," *Futurist* 15 (August 1981): 44.
23. Goodman, "Helper Bank," 398.
24. *Aging Alone: A Report of the Commonwealth Fund Commission on Elderly People Living Alone* (Baltimore: The Commonwealth Fund, 1988), 53. This report defines serious chronic health problems as arthritis, hypertension, and vision and hearing problems. Data was supplied from National Center for Health Statistics.
25. Quoted in Barbara Hershberger, "Living in the Freedom There Is," *Activities, Adaptation & Aging* 2 (Fall 1981): 51.

Volunteerism

Chapter 1

An Overview of Volunteerism

FACTS OF INTEREST

- The value of organized volunteer service is $150 billion a year
- Virtually every facet of human affairs offers volunteer opportunities
- More than half of those who volunteer say they do it because they want to do something useful to help others
- About 40 percent of U.S. citizens aged 65 to 74, and 29 percent of those over age 75 are volunteers
- The majority of volunteers over age 65 contribute time to religious organizations

This chapter examines the many dimensions of volunteerism in the United States. It includes statistical information, an overview of the areas where volunteers serve, and information on how individuals integrate volunteerism into their lives.

The Who, When, What, and Where of Volunteerism

The facts and figures in this section provide a backdrop for understanding the significance of volunteer service in modern U.S. culture. Much of this information was drawn from Independent

Sector's definitive survey, *Giving and Volunteering in the United States: Findings from a National Survey,* hereinafter referred to as the IS Survey.[1]

Who Volunteers?

A number of recent studies have assessed volunteer activity among older adults. According to the IS survey, 40 percent of those aged 65 to 74 and 29 percent of those over age 75 volunteer. Combined, these percentages represent more than 11 million adults age 65-plus. A 1988 survey[2] conducted by the American Association of Retired Persons (AARP) reported even greater volunteer participation, 41 percent, among those age 75 and over. A study by the U.S. Bureau of Labor Statistics indicated a 17 percent level of voluntary activity among the age 65-plus population.[3] However, this study was not specifically focused on volunteerism; the data on voluntary activity were drawn from supplemental questions.

How Much Time Do Volunteers Give?

On an average, volunteers age 65 to 74 give 6 hours a week, compared to an average of 4.7 hours for all volunteers over age 18. Volunteers age 75 and over average 4.4 hours per week. The IS survey found that a significant portion of volunteers in all age groups were contributing more hours than in earlier surveys. A 1988 AARP survey reports that respondents in the 60-plus age group "appear to give more time per month for their volunteer activities than those under 60." In the age 60 to 74 category, almost 20 percent of the respondents reported spending 5 to 10 hours per week in volunteer work.[4] Clearly, the 65-plus age group contributes at least 20 percent more time to volunteer service than other age groups in the population.

What Is the Dollar Value of Volunteer Service?

According to the IS Survey, the estimated dollar value of volunteer time donated to organized service activities in 1988 was $150 billion. The figure would be far greater had estimates been included for informal service, which comprises 40 percent of volunteer activity. The survey classified as informal such tasks as baby-sitting, assisting the elderly and handicapped, assisting a paid professional, and acting as a trustee of an organization.

Where Do Volunteers Give Their Time?

Religious organizations garner the greatest share of volunteer effort in all age groups. In 1985 the Independent Sector reported that, of all adults age 65-plus, 25 percent contributed time to religious organizations. In a 1981 AARP survey of 55-plus adults, 66 percent of the volunteers did volunteer work related to religious organizations. Forty-two percent worked in community-service agencies, 27 percent in social-service agencies, and 20 percent in youth-service organizations.[5]

The Scope of Volunteerism in American Society

Volunteerism is present in every conceivable facet of American life, including the following:

Provision of food, clothing, and shelter

Education

Science

Civic affairs

Spiritual development

Health

Economic development

The physical environment

Religion

Politics

Government

Safety

Human relationships

The arts

Recreation

Volunteer-service activity in the United States falls into eight major areas: the public sector; political action; the nonprofit, independent sector; informal service; corporate volunteer programs; community/public access television; volunteer-service banks; and self-help groups. Most volunteer activities are in the first four areas, which have been established for many years. The latter four areas, while relatively recent developments, show promise of continuing growth.

The Public Sector

Municipal, county, state, and federal government agencies rely on volunteer support to augment the services supported by tax revenues. In Oskaloosa, Iowa, for example, the Mahaska County Historical Society operates the Nelson Pioneer Farm, a museum dedicated to the history of the early farmer. Volunteers help in many aspects of the project, working as tour guides and maintaining the 14 buildings on the site.

The following are some of the other ways in which volunteers can participate in the operations of public-sector agencies:

Advisory boards

Airport information booths

Art work

Clerical work

College-program assistance and development

Computer work

Conservation projects

Cooking

Courtroom assistance

Crime-victim assistance

Disaster relief

Economic-development projects

Filmmaking

Firefighting and prevention

Gardening

Historical landmark refurbishment and maintenance

Hospital emergency-room patient and family support

Library assistance

Mediation and arbitration

Museum work

National forest and park maintenance

Neighborhood-crime prevention

Parole programs

Photography

Police assistance

Policy-planning groups

Public-grounds maintenance

Public-school program assistance and development

Radio-program development and production

Recreation programs

Research projects

Search-and-rescue operations

Senior-citizen programs

Speakers' bureaus

Sports-event traffic control and ushering

Telephone hotlines

Television programming and production

Tour guidance

Tourist-attraction maintenance and staffing

Ushering at civic events

Visitor information bureaus

Writing of technical, documentary, brochure, feature, and historical material

Youth programs

Zoo maintenance

Political Action

Volunteers are an essential part of every election effort. No candidate can get elected, no ordinance or bond election can pass without the contribution of thousands of hours from volunteers whose diverse skills support every phase of the political process. Individuals may contribute their services to a political party, a particular candidate, or a specific issue, cause, or organization. They may work informally, either alone or in conjunction with a few other persons, or formally, through affiliation with an organized group such as a political party, an organization, or an institution.

Political activities that depend partly or wholly on volunteer efforts include the following:

Get-out-the-vote campaigns—phoning, mailing, canvassing, transportation, informing the citizenry, assistance at the polls

Promoting citizen involvement—voter-registration work, voter education

Fund-raising—public speaking, letter writing, planning and organizing events

Direct candidate assistance—speech, campaign, and press materials development; issues research; arrangement of public appearances

Participation in the legislative process—letters and calls to elected officials, collaboration with elected officials in drafting legislation and policy positions

The Nonprofit, Independent Sector

This is the area where the majority of volunteer hours are contributed. According to John W. Gardner, the nonprofit segment of the private sector has been variously named the "voluntary sector," the "third sector," or most recently, the "independent sector."[6]

Included in this category are organizations and institutions incorporated under the federal tax statutes as tax-exempt and nonprofit.[7] Among these are libraries, museums, religious organizations, schools and colleges, charitable organizations, health and welfare agencies, citizen action groups, neighborhood organizations, self-help groups, professional-development societies, social-service agencies, and artistic and cultural organizations.

Virtually every volunteer opportunity that exists in the public sector also exists in the nonprofit sector (see list on page 24). Those options, along with the following, represent only a portion of the service opportunities available through nonprofit organizations.

Abortion issues

Adult education

Animal protection

Civil rights

Consumer protection

Day-care assistance for adults and children

Domestic-violence prevention and reduction

Drug- and alcohol-abuse recovery

Environmental protection and beautification

Ethics

Family planning

Gun control and rights to bear arms

Ham-radio operation

Historic preservation

Human rights

Hunger relief

Literacy

Mental health

Minority rights

Peer counseling

Performing arts

Physical health

Political reform

Professional development

Respite for care givers

Self-help groups

Senior citizen concerns

Spiritual development

Support groups

Telephone reassurance

Third World development

Tutoring

Voter registration and education

Women's issues

Informal Volunteer Service

According to the IS survey, 40 percent of volunteer service is "informal," that is, conducted outside the structure of organized programs. Because informal service is usually person-to-person, it is undoubtedly underrepresented in polls and surveys and often is not even acknowledged by the giver as an act of volunteerism.

One example of informal volunteer service is that of Reverend Edgar Wahlberg, age 86, who translated his concern about the success of peace talks between the United States and the Soviet Union into a booklet, *A Concern for Humanity*. Wahlberg sent copies of the booklet to President Ronald Reagan, Soviet leader Mikhail Gorbachev, and many others around the nation and the world.

Another example of informal service is Helen Finner's mentor program for young mothers called "Mama Said." She matched experienced mothers in a Chicago housing project with young women who needed parenting skills. "If I save only 10 or 15 young mothers—turn their lives around—then I will feel that what I'm doing is not in vain," she said.

Informal service often takes place between friends or acquaintances and can lead to strong bonds between giver and receiver. The following are some typical examples of informal volunteer services:

Adopt-a-Family

Baby-sitting

Bill paying

Companionship

Cooking

Errands

Financial support

Friendly visiting

Handyman services

Housecleaning

House-sitting

Insurance claims filing

Laundry

Letter writing

Locating services

Pet care

Reading to the visually impaired

Respite for care givers

Shopping

Transportation

Yard maintenance

Employer-Sponsored Volunteer Programs

Increasingly, corporations, businesses, and government agencies are encouraging and supporting organized volunteer activities among their employees and retirees. More than 600 corporations have such programs.[8] Leaders in this movement are AT&T, Levi Strauss, The Travelers, General Mills, and ARCO.

Corporate-retiree volunteer groups form a powerful force in many communities by carving their own service niches and by teaming up with other programs. A typical project provides home maintenance for the needy, with retirees donating the labor and know-how, and the company contributing the materials. Often such corporate programs focus on a special need. For example, the Telephone Pioneers, retirees of AT&T and other telephone companies, are known for their inventions and designs of sports equipment for the disabled. A leader among public-sector retiree programs is the National Association of Retired Federal Employees (NARFE), whose multiple objectives include the promotion and recognition of volunteerism among its members.

In 1986 the Junior League of Minneapolis and several of the pioneering corporate programs formed the National Retiree Volunteer Center (NRVC).[9] NRVC's purpose is to help employers mobilize the resources of retirees for leadership and service in meeting community needs. NRVC's membership includes a growing list of both private- and public-sector employers.

Community Access and Cable Television

Volunteer jobs exist in community and regional television stations throughout the United States. The programs are managed differently in each location, but the following general description applies in most instances.

COMMUNITY/PUBLIC ACCESS TELEVISION STATIONS (C/PAS)

These stations exist in many communities that brought in cable television franchises after 1976. C/PAS's usually exist because communities require them as a condition of the cable company's franchise. The cable television companies provide the funds to operate the C/PAS, which are available for programming by any individual or group in the community. No commercial or pornographic programs are allowed.

C/PAS's have a variety of administrative structures. Some are operated by nonprofit corporations set up by municipal governments. Others are operated by the cable companies themselves. In some communities, responsibility for operating the C/PAS is assigned to an institution such as a library, a school district, or a university.

Typical C/PAS programs include interviews on social issues, documentaries on community history and the lives of interesting local figures, how-to information with a local flavor such as gardening techniques, shows for children, and information programs on community events.

VOLUNTEER OPPORTUNITIES IN C/PAS

Volunteers work in all aspects of program production. Technical crews operate the cameras, set up the sound and lighting systems, arrange the props, and design makeup and costumes. Production aspects include script writing, background research, invitation and scheduling of guests, and program direction. Program producers oversee and coordinate the entire show. Aspiring producers either recruit their own technical and production crews or work through the C/PAS to assemble crews from its trainees.

The cable television company provides the equipment, studio facilities, and some professional staff assistance. Individuals and groups may use these at no cost to themselves. All work is done on a voluntary basis. Those who use the equipment must demonstrate knowledge of its operation either through prior training or attendance at C/PAS-sponsored training. The staff acts as consultants and trainers for the volunteers, some of whom bring prior experience and skills to the jobs, and others learn as they go. One C/PAS director says many volunteers who start by learning how to operate the equipment find that they want to move on to other aspects of programming such as directing or producing shows.

Additional information about volunteer opportunities in C/PAS is available by contacting the local cable television company or by calling the cable communications officer in the city government.

Special Categories of Volunteer Service

The following modes of service partially fit the definition of volunteerism, in that aid is freely given without monetary payment. But these volunteer activities also include some elements of barter because services are traded without the exchange of money.

VOLUNTEER-SERVICE BANKS

In a service bank, individuals provide services for which they receive units of credit. They can then use the credit for themselves, or in some cases transfer credits to others. For example, an individual might accumulate credits by doing lawn care, transportation, and home-maintenance tasks for needy elders. In the event of an illness or accident, he could use his credits to "purchase" services such as cooking, housecleaning, and laundry until he regains the strength for these activities.[10]

SELF-HELP GROUPS

These are informal groups run by members, who share a common problem or goal. Their purpose is to extend mutual support and to exchange information about resources and coping strategies. Alcoholics Anonymous is a classic example of the self-help group. The still-growing self-help movement encompasses scores of concerns, including the care of aged relatives, stroke recovery, life-style change, mutual support by AIDS victims and families, and professional development.

Many groups emerge because individuals cannot find support for a particular problem. For example, Donna Oettinger formed a support group in New Jersey for herself and others who suffered from neurofibromatosis or Elephant Man's disease. "We help each other to cope and accept the disease. . . . For the first time in my life, I can honestly say that I have friends."

The self-help movement's distinguishing characteristic is that groups operate on their own initiatives without professional guidance. Some groups assemble regularly, others irregularly. Some maintain contact by phone, mail, or computer networks. For further information, see the summary of the Self-Help Clearinghouse in Chapter 4.[11]

Integrating Volunteerism into Daily Life

Time Commitments

As mentioned earlier in this chapter, the average amount of volunteer service per individual is three-and-a-half hours a week. The actual amount of service, however, varies widely, depending on personal schedules, the nature of the service, or the skills an individual contributes. The following are some examples of different patterns of time commitment:

Regular activities on a daily, weekly, or monthly schedule. Examples: conducting a story hour at the library on Tuesdays, Thursdays, and Saturdays; or staffing the information booth at the municipal airport the second and fourth Wednesdays of every month.

Occasional service. This often applies for individuals who have special expertise. Examples: consultation by a horticulturalist with community gardeners on pest control, counseling for crime victims, or tutoring on a particular topic.

Seasonal volunteer work. Examples: participation in fund-raising campaigns, preparing holiday dinners for the homeless, or agricultural gleaning programs.

On-call service. This is sometimes necessary because of the nature of the work. Examples: ham-radio operators who assist with communication in flood or earthquake situations, volunteer fire fighters, or search-and-rescue teams.

Regular participation in scheduled, short-term events. Examples: fund-raising, civic programs, theater projects, holiday programs.

Project assignments with commitment to a partial or entire task. Examples: chairing a building program, coordinating a bake sale, conducting or assisting at a workshop, serving a term of office, or designing a computer program.

Multiple Volunteer Commitments

According to the IS Survey, on an average, persons who volunteer engage in more than two voluntary assignments a year. Dividing one's efforts offers such advantages as the opportunity to express different values—conservation of natural resources and a love of children, for example—or satisfaction of a variety of interests. Working at different jobs can also help volunteers balance the demands on their personal energy. For example, if working in a rehabilitation hospital is fascinating yet exhausting, doing routine data entry on a computer several hours a week could provide a needed respite. Similarly, a person who performs one volunteer service out of a sense of obligation might balance it with another one chosen because of personal interest.

Some volunteer work requires a heavy financial investment, such as a volunteer vacation to a developing country, where volunteers pay their own expenses and help citizens with local projects. An individual might choose to combine one such project with others that are more affordable.

Large versus Small Volunteer Organizations

Millions of service hours are delivered through giant national and international service organizations such as the American Association of Retired Persons (AARP), the National Council of Jewish Women, the Red Cross, the Salvation Army, the Young Men's Christian Association (YMCA), and the Young Women's Christian Association (YWCA). Other millions of hours go to smaller organizations—churches, neighborhood groups, local nonprofit, and governmental agencies.

Each type of organization has its appeal. Large ones tend to have clearly defined policies and formalized structures. They offer opportunities for regional and national leadership positions, organized training, and travel to conferences and conventions.

Small organizations generally have local control and flexible structure. They provide opportunities for variety and decision-making within the individual volunteer jobs, as well as favorable climates for innovation.

Types of Volunteer Contributions

Time, personal energy, and skills are the resources most commonly donated by volunteers. Other contributions include the use of personal belongings such as cars, computers, card tables, chairs, kitchen utensils, electronic equipment, tools, and buildings. Volunteers often donate such consumable items as food, fabrics, building materials, and office supplies. They might donate the equipment necessary to provide services; for instance, tape recorders, trucks, lights, or conference-room furnishings.

Many volunteers also donate money, either in the form of straight contributions or in conjunction with other goods or services. The IS Survey found that volunteers were more likely to make financial contributions than nonvolunteers, with 56 percent of volunteers giving money, compared to 44 percent of nonvolunteers. The volunteers showed a tendency to donate money in the same areas where they donated time.

Expenses of Volunteering

Volunteer work can involve expenses. Note the following examples:

Transportation to and from the job

Meals away from home

Lodging away from home

Incidentals while living away from home

Insurance

Special clothing

Special equipment and supplies

Long-distance phone calls

Training

Coverages of expenses lies along a continuum that ranges from "sponsoring organization pays for all" to "volunteer pays for all." Training is the only requisite of volunteering that service programs usually furnish at no cost to the volunteer, although in some cases volunteers may be required to pay for training expenses as well.

Geographic Locations of Volunteer Service

Volunteer work may be performed anywhere, from the volunteer's home to locations around the world. For example, one couple participated in an arrangement where each morning at eight o'clock one of them dialed the phone number of an elderly friend. After two rings they hung up and listened for the answering two rings that would assure them that their friend was safe and well. Workers for Volunteers in Technical Assistance, on the other hand, take assignments in such countries as Lusaka, Zambia, and Kenya.

The following are further examples of this wide array of geographic options:

In-home volunteer service
Telephone calling

Needlework

Baby-sitting

Tutoring

Computer work

Cooking for individuals or community events

Fact finding

Writing brochures, letters, or other kinds of materials

Close-to-home or neighborhood service
Canvassing for political issues or candidates

Shopping and other neighborly help

Participation in neighborhood associations

Crime prevention

Friendly visiting

Assistance in the schools

Neighborhood beautification

Recycling newspapers, cans, glass bottles

Adopt-a-family, adopt-a-grandchild projects

Service within the community
Food banks

Libraries

Public radio and television stations

Church work

Board and committee service

Governmental organizations

Involvement in nonprofit organizations

Service projects sponsored by corporations, labor unions, radio stations or newspapers, and for-profit organizations

Service within the state
Park maintenance

Disaster relief

Speaking and teaching assignments

Consulting on community projects, such as building community centers, preserving historic sites, tourism, research, or replicating successful programs from other locations

National service
Community-service programs, usually government sponsored, ranging in length from several days to several months

Consultation on public works or nonprofit programs

Volunteer vacations in which volunteers pay their expenses and work on nonprofit, church- or government-sponsored programs

International service
Work sponsored by churches and religiously oriented organizations, nonprofit groups, and government agencies

Consultation, research, or direct service to communities and individuals

Crisis-oriented service, disaster relief, education, economic development, research, or conservation

Structure of Volunteer Jobs

Volunteer jobs vary widely in structure. The highly structured ones have job descriptions and require extensive orientation. An example is telephone work in the Red Cross' disaster-relief programs. Others are spontaneous and informal, such as clearing the snow off a neighbor's walk while the neighbor tends to a sick relative. Following are examples of the ways in which volunteer tasks are organized and accomplished.

Job descriptions that prescribe tasks and responsibilities for the individual. Examples: treasurer, coach, or usher.

Jobs designed by a volunteer—independently or within an organization—to address an unmet need or to make use of special volunteer expertise or interest. Examples: conducting an oral-history project at a nursing home, or expanding a Meals-on-Wheels program to include delivery of library materials.

Contribution of special expertise upon request as needed, much like consulting in for-profit organizations. Examples: developing filing or inventory systems, reviewing bylaws or contracts for legal snags, or consultation on designing a set of theatrical props.

Direct service to clients of a program or organization. Examples: serving meals at a shelter for the homeless, planting trees in a reforestation project, or teaching job-search skills to young adults.

Indirect or support service behind the scenes that enables or enhances direct service. Examples: fund-raising, clerical work, public relations, or volunteer training.

Motives for Volunteering and Not Volunteering

According to the IS Survey, only one out of four respondents of all ages said they refused to volunteer when asked. In the 65-plus age group, 24 percent of the refusers cited "lack of time/too busy" as their reason; 38 percent gave health reasons.[12]

Respondents age 65 and over gave the following reasons for first becoming involved in volunteer work. The total exceeds 100 percent because many respondents gave more than one reason.

1. Wanted to do something useful (56 percent)

2. Thought I would enjoy the work (40 percent)

3. Religious concerns (27 percent)

4. Had a lot of free time (14 percent)

Volunteers continued to work for the same reasons they started, with one notable exception: "interest in the activity" replaced "had a lot of free time" as a motivation.

1. Like doing something useful (53 percent)

2. Enjoy doing the work (39 percent)

3. Religious concerns (30 percent)

4. Interest in the activity (28 percent)

The AARP survey[13] reported that 14 percent of respondents over age 65 said that "keeping me active" was a reason for their volunteer service. Another motive of many volunteers is "to repay some of the goodnesses that have come my way."

The following comments offer personal views of the volunteer spirit indicated by the surveys:

Brian O'Connell wrote, in his essay *The Meaning of Volunteering,* [14] "Whether we want to express the meaning of service in involved ways or prefer simpler forms doesn't really matter. It can be charity or enlightened self-interest or people's humanity to people. These are all ways of describing why we volunteer, why volunteering provides some of our happiest moments, and why the good that we do lives after us."

"[It] gives me a reason to wake up each morning. My life has such meaning! It feels so good to give of myself to others." [15]

"At one time I needed [help] from the local community services and now I'm helping them." [16]

"It's for our church and I think it comes first." [17]

"Many pleasures in life tend to wear out, but the pleasure of helping others stays with us always. I can't believe [it] can mean so much to me . . . knowing that I am really making others' lives a little better. In helping others, I am helped, too." [18]

Notes

1. *Giving and Volunteering in the United States: Findings from a National Survey,* 1988 edition (Washington, DC: Independent Sector, 1988). Independent Sector commissioned the Gallup Organization to conduct this study in 1988. It is to be conducted every two years. The purpose is to establish trend information on the financial-giving and volunteering behavior of the U.S. population. The respondents were a nationally representative sample of 2,775 persons age 18 and older.

2. *Attitudes of Americans over 45 Years of Age on Volunteerism* (Washington, DC: American Association of Retired Persons, 1988), the study was prepared by Hamilton, Frederick & Schneiders.

3. "Thirty-Eight Million Persons Do Volunteer Work," USDL 90-154, 3 (Washington, DC: U.S. Department of Labor, Bureau of Labor Statistics, 1990). These figures on volunteerism were drawn from a 1989 Current Population Survey (CPS) of households rather than individuals. The CPS sample was based on 1980 census figures, which were updated with the most current information available to the Department of Labor at the time of the study.

4. *Attitudes of Americans,* 8.

5. Carole Allan, *Retirees: A Profile of the 55-and-Over Market* (Alexandria, VA: United Way of America, 1984), 26.

6. Brian O'Connell, ed., *America's Voluntary Spirit: A Book of Readings* (New York: The Foundation Center, 1983), ix.

7. For further information on such organizations, please see the listing for *Charitable Contributions* in the Booklets, Manuals, and Pamphlets section of Chapter 5, or call the local IRS office.

8. *Retirees: A Profile of the 55-and-Over Market* (Alexandria, VA: United Way of America, 1988), 27.

9. Please refer to the listing for the National Retiree Volunteer Center in Chapter 4 for further information.

10. Catherine Goodman Chase, "Helper Bank: A Reciprocal Services Program for Older Adults," *Social Work* 29 (July/August 1984): 397.

11. Carla Cantor, "Support Groups Fill Emotional Gaps," *New York Times,* 28 September 1986, sec. 1.

12. *Giving and Volunteering,* 35.

13. *Attitudes of Americans,* 6.

14. O'Connell, ed., *America's Voluntary Spirit,* 408.

15. *The Retired Senior Volunteer Program: A Manual for Planning, Implementing and Operating RSVP* (Washington, DC: American Association for International Aging, 1988), 1.

16. *Attitudes of Americans,* Appendix B, 2.

17. Ibid.

18. *The Senior Companion Program: A Manual for Planning, Implementing and Operating the Senior Companion Program* (Washington, DC: American Association for International Aging, 1988), 1.

Chapter 2

Finding Volunteer Opportunities

- There is a volunteer job to match virtually any interest and skill

- Volunteer work can be done on mountain tops, in foreign countries, and even from nursing-home beds

- Choosing volunteer work on the basis of personal interests and favorite skills increases the chances for fulfillment and productivity

The steps for finding a rewarding volunteer job are similar to those used in finding a paid job. This chapter offers a practical, systematic approach to finding volunteer opportunities to match any individual's skills, interests, and circumstances.

The process can be divided into two parts:

1. Self-assessment—this is an evaluation process used to determine what sort of work will best fulfill the potential volunteer's interests, skills, and expectations

2. Identifying or creating a specific volunteer job(s) that matches those interests, skills, and expectations and that fits with the individual's particular circumstances

Self-Assessment: The Cornerstone for a Good Match

A thorough self-assessment is the key to finding satisfaction in volunteer work, and it can be an enjoyable process of discovery as well. It consists of three steps:

1. Identifying personal interests and/or values that one would like to express through volunteer work.

2. Identifying the skills one would most like to use in volunteer work. These may be skills honed through years of career and life experience or new skills one would like to acquire, either for personal satisfaction or in order to qualify for future paid employment.

3. Identifying the rewards one expects to receive from volunteer work.

Step One: Identify Personal Interests

Sometimes the choice of volunteer work may grow out of a powerful experience or deep personal conviction. In 1975, Lois Hess lost her 24-year-old son to a bullet from an escaped convict's handgun. She turned her grief into a crusade against the sale of cheap handguns. Thirteen years later she saw the results of her efforts when Maryland voters approved a ban on the sale of the weapons.

Other times, volunteer service grows from long-cherished dreams. At the age of 63, Marie St. Germain modeled, for the first time, in a fashion show at a local fund-raising event. Now she frequently appears in clothing shows at various community events. St. Germain had almost forgotten about her desire to be a model during her years as a mother and homemaker. After her husband died, she decided to make her dream part of the new chapter of her life. "Helping others by doing something I've always wanted to do—what more could I ask?" she said.

For still others, the ideal volunteer job comes out of a serendipitous discovery. Jo Cox was a seamstress and typist until she was 64. She wanted to do something entirely different when she retired, but did not have a clear goal. When she happened to see a notice for a clowning workshop, she remembered how intrigued she had always been with her father's and grand-father's careers as stage performers and decided to enroll in the workshop. "The first night I felt as though I'd come home," she recalls. Cox perfected her routines as a volunteer in nursing homes and in a wide variety of children's programs, and she now performs in professional clowning engagements in addition to her regular volunteer performances.

For these persons the choice of volunteer work was clear. Many people, however, need to go through a more systematic process in order to clarify their interests. Through this process individuals can identify one or more strong desires or interests, which become themes for their volunteer activities. For example, a minister was able to discover that the way for him to find fulfillment in his retirement work was to "talk and help people." He was able to use his resonant voice toward that end by record-ing written material for the blind.

A volunteer-service niche exists for nearly every personal interest. After identifying interests that might point to directions for volunteer service, the next step is to locate organizations or groups that sponsor activities related to those interests. Chapter 1 contains several lists of potential volunteer activities, particu-larly in the section entitled "The Scope of Volunteerism in Amer-ican Society" on page 23. Further ideas will be found in the lists that follow.

OPPORTUNITIES THROUGH NATIONAL ORGANIZATIONS

The following list contains a sampling of the hundreds of inter-ests or concerns that can become volunteer jobs. Under each interest are one or more national organizations whose activities address that interest. For descriptions of the organizations men-tioned here, see Chapter 4.

Aging successfully
National Council of Jewish Women

Alcohol- and drug-addiction recovery
Al-Anon

Alcoholics Anonymous (AA)

Salvation Army

Volunteers of America (VOA)

Alzheimer's disease research
Alzheimer's Disease and Related Disorders Association

National Association of Retired Federal Employees

Birth defects prevention and research
March of Dimes Birth Defects Foundation

Blood banks
American Red Cross

Cancer prevention, research, and aid to patients
American Cancer Society

Cardiopulmonary resuscitation (CPR) training
American Red Cross

Care of the terminally ill
Hospice Education Institute

Child-abuse prevention
National Committee for the Prevention of Child Abuse

National Exchange Club Foundation for the Prevention
of Child Abuse

Children and youth services
National Council of Jewish Women

Companionship to older adults
Senior Companion Program

Corporate volunteer service
National Retiree Volunteer Center

Criminal justice

American Association of Retired Persons (AARP)

National Association of Volunteers in Criminal Justice

Salvation Army

Day camps

Young Men's Christian Association (YMCA)

Defensive-driving training for older adults

AARP

Disaster relief

American Red Cross

Drunk-driving prevention and legislation

Mothers Against Drunk Driving (MADD)

Emergency clothing and food

Society of St. Vincent de Paul

Employment counseling

Young Women's Christian Association (YWCA)

Employment opportunities for older adults

AARP

Environmental protection and research

Earthwatch

National Arbor Day Foundation

Sierra Club

U.S. Forest Service

Eyesight preservation

Lions Club International

Family-violence prevention

Task Force on Families in Crisis

First-aid training
American Red Cross

Health benefits for the elderly
AARP

Heart disease prevention, research, and aid to patients
American Heart Association

Historic preservation
Association for Living Historical Farms and Agricultural Museums

Friends of the Cumbres & Toltec Scenic Railroad

National Association for the Preservation and Perpetuation of Storytelling (NAPPS)

Homelessness
National Coalition for the Homeless

Salvation Army

VOA

Housing
AARP (for older adults)

Gray Panthers

Immunization clinics
American Red Cross

Intergenerational programs
AARP

Foster Grandparents

Generations Together

Gray Panthers

International volunteer service
Global Volunteers

International Executive Service Corps

Peace Corps

Volunteers in Overseas Cooperative Assistance

Volunteers in Technical Assistance

Literacy
Laubach Literacy Action

Literacy Volunteers of America

Meals for the elderly
VOA

Mediation
AARP

National Center for Mediation Education

Mentoring
YMCA

Political action
AARP

Alzheimer's Disease and Related Disorders Association

Citizen Action

Common Cause

Gray Panthers

League of Women Voters of the United States

MADD

National AIDS Network

National Coalition for the Homeless

Older Women's League (OWL)

Sierra Club

Task Force on Families in Crisis

Political reform
Common Cause

Public radio and television
National Friends of Public Broadcasting

National Public Radio

Reminiscence
AARP

Respite for care givers
National Council of Catholic Women

School-volunteer service
National Association of Partners in Education

Screening clinics
American Red Cross

Self-help
AA

Al-Anon

Alzheimer's Disease and Related Disorders Association

Self-Help Clearinghouse

SHARE-USA

Services to the blind
Telephone Pioneers

Services to the handicapped
Lions Clubs

Telephone Pioneers

VOA

Small-business counseling
Service Corps of Retired Executives

Storytelling
NAPPS

Swimming
YMCA

Tax counseling and assistance for older adults
AARP

Transportation
AARP (for older adults)

American Red Cross

Unwed mothers' counseling
Salvation Army

Volunteer talent bank for older adults
AARP

Volunteer vacations
American Hiking Society

Friends of the Cumbres & Toltec Scenic Railroad

Global Volunteers

U.S. Forest Service

Voter education
Citizen Action

League of Women Voters of the United States

Voter registration
League of Women Voters of the United States

Project VOTE!

Water-safety training
American Red Cross

Widowed persons' services
(AARP) Widowed Persons Service

Wilderness or wildlife preservation
American Hiking Society

Sierra Club

U.S. Forest Service

Women's issues
National Council of Jewish Women

OWL

YWCA

LOCAL OPPORTUNITIES

The following list contains suggestions for addressing interests through local groups, institutions, or programs. Following each item are suggestions for groups or organized programs that might use such services.

Carpentry
Day-care centers

Nonprofit organizations

Child care
Shelters for the homeless

Battered women's shelters

Computer work
Nonprofit organizations

Government agencies

Fashion modeling
Fund-raisers for nonprofit organizations

Fire prevention
Fire department

Helping the frail elderly maintain homes or apartments
Churches

Neighborhood organizations

Historic preservation
State historical societies

Museums

Mentoring of the younger generation
Public schools

Youth clubs

Neighborhood crime prevention
Police department

Neighborhood association

Performing arts including theater, music, dance, comedy, and clowning
Community theaters

Orchestras

Civic events

Comedy clubs

Political action
Headquarters of political party of choice

Respite for care givers to ill family members
Hospices

Churches

Search-and-rescue operations
Civil air patrol

County search-and-rescue programs

Storytelling

Libraries

Schools

Support for cancer, AIDS, or Alzheimer's disease patients and their families

Hospitals

Hospices

Tutoring

Adult-literacy programs

Schools

Step Two: Narrow the Field to the Top Three Areas of Interest

Using the above lists and the list on page 23 in Chapter 1 as a starting point, select up to three interest areas or organizations that seem attractive. Then begin to explore the opportunities within each of those areas. This may lead to concentrated work within one area or diverse opportunities in two or even all three of the areas.

Some people are happiest concentrating their volunteer work in one area and looking for ways to expand within that area. For example, a volunteer in a shelter for family-violence victims might learn the skills necessary to staff a hotline for families in crisis, then get training in teaching families alternatives to violence.

Other individuals prefer to divide their energies and time among a variety of volunteer jobs. For example, working backstage in a community theater can offset the intensity of co-facilitating a support group for care givers to ill family members.

Step Three: Identify Skill Preferences

Every person who reaches middle age has a large body of skills, knowledge, and talents. The next step in the process is to evaluate the available skills in light of the chosen interest areas. These should be skills that are pleasurable, interesting, and/or challenging to use, not just things one is "good at." For example, a woman who is an excellent cook might be happier diagnosing problems and making repairs on household appliances.

A common pitfall is to think that the only useful skills for volunteer service are those that are highly developed or that have been used in paid jobs. While the person who enjoys using skills developed over time will find ideas for transplanting those skills to volunteer settings, others will find ways to learn and refine new skills through volunteer work.

Almost every service area offers a wide range of possible skill applications, with allowances for personal circumstances and energy levels. A volunteer with an interest in wilderness preservation, for example, could climb mountains to gather environmental data, participate in a footrace or a walkathon to raise money, give lectures to service clubs and elementary-school students to raise awareness, take photographs for publications and brochures, or put labels on fund-raising mail.

Investing time and thought in choosing which skills to use is as crucial to productivity and enjoyment in volunteer service as it is in paid employment. The following information offers guidance for this step in the self-assessment process.

GENERAL SKILL CATEGORIES

Skills fall into three categories, according to life-planning expert Richard Bolles:[1]

1. Skills with people

2. Skills with information or data

3. Skills with things

People skills may involve "all kinds of people, or very specific kinds of people—defined by age, culture, background, kinds of problems they face, etc."[2] Working with animals also falls within this category.

A few examples of people-skill applications are helping adults find solutions to their problems, teaching children to swim, getting along with difficult people, overcoming language barriers, telephone work, counseling, public speaking, helping others to feel at ease, and training animals.

Information or data skills involve "information, knowledge, data, ideas, facts, figures, statistics, etc."[3] Information skills could entail planning and organizing, estimating the amount of money necessary to complete a project, writing, seeing new applications for existing ideas, keeping track of details, interior decorating, card playing, researching, and observing/recording.

Skill with things can involve "physical objects, instruments, tools, machinery, equipment, vehicles, materials, and desktop items such as pencils, paper clips, telephones, stamps, etc."[4] A sampling of this skill category includes "using one's body as an instrument of accomplishment," as in dancing. A few examples of skills in this category are precision woodworking, making repairs, needlework, making music, hiking, gardening, photography, sailing, and drawing.

NARROWING THE FIELD TO THE TOP SKILL PREFERENCES

Start by prioritizing the three skill categories according to preference. For example, working with information might be number one; working with people, number two; and working with things, number three.

It would be helpful to ask: As a volunteer, how do I want to divide my time among the skill categories? Some individuals clearly prefer to spend all their time using one skill category, such as working with people nearly 100 percent of the time. Others would rather divide their time among two or three skill categories; for instance, 50 percent of the time working with things, 30 percent with information, and 20 percent with people.

There are thousands of ways to work within each skill category. Singling out the applications that hold the most personal appeal increases the chances of finding or creating a fulfilling volunteer niche. Following are some examples of ways to work within each of the three skill categories.

Working with people

Young, old

Females, males

Illiterate, well-educated

Terminally ill

Individuals, groups

Handicapped

Incarcerated

Teaching

Serving

Entertaining

Leading

Working with information or data

Reading blueprints

Interpreting standards

Writing computer software manuals

Adapting recipes

Bookkeeping

Testing safety procedures

Collecting historical data

Designing planning surveys

Working with things or objects

Repairing

Building

Organizing

Operating

Maintaining

Inventing

Adapting

Testing

Moving

USING CURRENT SKILLS, ACQUIRING NEW ONES

Many people find ways to build on current skills and acquire new ones in the course of their volunteer work; thus, they are creating new opportunities. Lewis Gebbe retired at age 60 from a middle-management career in the petroleum industry. At an exhibition sponsored by social-service agencies, Gebbe talked to a nurse from the community visiting-nurse association about the needs of men with long-term illnesses. Knowing he had found his challenge, Gebbe became certified as a nurse's aide and developed a special interest in, and ability for working with, terminally ill men. He offered regular respite care so their families would have time to go to work and tend to other matters. As he became known for his skills in working with these patients, the visiting-nurse association began inviting him to give presentations at professional-education meetings.

Virginia Spray of Burden, Kansas, transferred skills polished during 27 years of elementary-school teaching experience to her new work as a Peace Corps volunteer. She joined the corps at age 71 and was assigned to Liberia, where she conducted teacher-training workshops. Later she helped a former Peace Corps volunteer develop textbooks for the Liberian students.

Step Four: Identify Desired Rewards

In a 1988 survey by AARP, 42 percent of respondents identified "personal enjoyment/fulfillment" as their main reason for volunteering.[5] Personal enjoyment/fulfillment represents different things for different people. Having a clear picture of the types of fulfillment or rewards one seeks from volunteer service is essential to choosing a job that can provide them.

Intangible rewards include personal growth, the satisfaction of being needed, productive use of time, fulfillment of a long-held dream, a chance to repay services received in the past, and the opportunity to bring joy to the lives of others. Retired engineer George Sable of Minneapolis, Minnesota, turned away lucrative consulting offers and chose instead to adapt equipment for disabled children and adults. His innovations include a hand-pedaled bicycle and a brace for an artist's arthritic hand. After designing his first bicycle, Sable said, "To see the smiles on these kids' faces, that's all I needed. I decided to do whatever I could to help."[6]

Other rewards for volunteer service include opportunities for refining skills or learning new ones, the chance to remain physically active, travel, new experiences, social contacts and friendships, employment leads and opportunities, maintaining mental fitness, access to office equipment, use of physical-fitness facilities, tuition-free classes, free or discounted admission to community events, equipment loans, and merchandise discounts. For a discussion of ways in which volunteer service can be used in exchange for goods or services, see Chapter 1.

Volunteer Job Sketches

The following sample sketches of volunteer jobs illustrate how the self-assessment steps described above can lead to a match between the person and the job.

SEVERAL JOBS YEILD DESIRED REWARDS

Kathryn Smith is a 72-year-old widow who lives in a senior citizens' high-rise apartment building and enjoys robust health. In her self-assessment, she identified her primary interest as helping frail elderly people maintain independent living, and she wants to use her skills at operating equipment and helping people feel at ease. She is seeking to use her time productively and to stay physically active, and she would like to work 30 hours a week, with four weeks off each year for family visits and vacations.

With this understanding, Mrs. Smith found a formal volunteer job with the local Red Cross chapter driving people to doctors' appointments. She also works on an informal basis doing grocery shopping and other essential errands for three frail elders who live in their own homes.

VOLUNTEERING DESPITE PHYSICAL LIMITATIONS

Sam Jones, age 65, lives at home with his wife, and has a heart condition that limits his physical activity. He identified a strong interest in helping to prevent high-school students from dropping out. He wanted to use his teaching skills and sought the rewards of being needed and using his time productively. He was able to work three to five hours a week. Mr. Jones decided to work in his own home as a reading tutor for one ninth grader from the local high school each semester and during the summer months.

Making the Match: Finding and Creating Volunteer Jobs

The following are some tips for locating and creating volunteer jobs within agencies and organizations. Finding the right volunteer job often requires several contacts and considerable persistence. This process itself can be a learning opportunity and a pathway to unexpected discoveries.

1. Browse through the listings in Chapter 4 to get an overview of the opportunities and needs for service. Contact the central headquarters of organizations for information. Check the phone directory for listings of local chapters.

2. Use the interest lists on pages 45 and 52 to identify national organizations or local contacts that might address your chosen interest areas.

3. Refer to the Index in the back of this book to locate specific types of organizations and resources.

4. Check sources of information in the local community: bulletin boards; literature racks; radio interviews and talk shows; locally produced television interview programs; daily and weekly newspapers, especially the feature pages for stories and calendars of service events; churches; hospitals; prisons; libraries; day-care centers; police and fire departments; public and community radio and television stations; senior citizen centers; state and municipally operated tourist attractions; prisons; museums; central clearinghouses of volunteer job listings; the Yellow Pages listings of

Associations, Organizations, Human Service
Organizations, and Social Service Organizations; the
courthouse; public schools; nursing homes; the public
parks and recreation department; former employers;
trade unions; and fraternal organizations.

5. Spread the word. Build a network. Ask friends and
relatives about their volunteer involvements and
whether they or their friends know of openings. An
advantage to this method of locating a volunteer job
is the chance to get a preview of the organization or
agency. Increase the possibilities for information by
stretching the network. Ask the doctor, dentist,
minister, pastor, rabbi, accountant, attorney, bus
driver, or veterinarian about ideas for service work.

6. When making contacts with programs, check for the
following signs of a high-quality work setting:

The staff appears eager to have volunteers on board

The staff makes an effort to match volunteer interests
and skills with jobs

Volunteer job descriptions are available

Orientation and periodic training for volunteers are
standard operating procedure

Volunteer-supervision policies are clearly defined

Volunteer-performance reviews are standard operating
procedure

Volunteer turnover is low

The staff will consider arranging trial periods before
placing volunteers in long-term positions

One's desired rewards for service are achievable or
negotiable within the program

Both volunteers and staff seem to enjoy their jobs and
work cooperatively with one another

Creating Volunteer Jobs in Established Programs

The information above refers primarily to situations in which volunteer jobs are already in place. Many needs exist that fall outside the realm of structured volunteer jobs. These, too, can offer opportunities for valuable and deeply satisfying service. Staff members are often open to volunteers' ideas for creating jobs to meet these needs. While they themselves might be too busy with the daily routine to plan the jobs, they are often willing to develop ideas with volunteers who take the initiative.

United States Forest Service (USFS) volunteer coordinator Lynn Young says that many of their most innovative volunteer programs stem from volunteer suggestions. "When we sit down and talk with people, all kinds of neat ideas can come up." He told of a summer volunteer who noticed the frequent loss and poor maintenance of the USFS' hand tools. One winter, the man returned to Colorado from Texas and lived in his motor home while he worked with the tools. He repaired them, then established an inventory and check-out system so they would be ready for use the next season. Said Young, "He filled a need, which our staff didn't have the time to handle."

At the University of Maryland[7] retired physicists Milton and Zaka Slawsky began informal tutoring for physics students and were soon joined by four other retired physicists. Eventually they formed a clinic that served 500 students each semester. The combined time contribution of the six physicists was 100 hours a week.

Some volunteer directors prefer to build jobs around demonstrated volunteer skills and preferences rather than go out and recruit people to fill prescribed slots. For example, the volunteer director for a ballet company said, "Come in and work with us for a while. You don't have to know anything about ballet to help us. As we get to know you, we'll help you find a project you like."

Creating Independent Volunteer Jobs

Some individuals create their own volunteer jobs by seeing a need and channeling their skills and energies to meet it. Annie Dodge Wauneka, for instance, started to educate members of her Navajo Indian tribe on the care of tuberculosis victims in the

1950s. At age 79 she was still teaching her people on the Arizona reservation. Her topic had changed to alcoholism, the leading killer of tribal members.[8]

Phoebe English found ways to serve others even though she needed volunteer assistance to carry out some of her own daily activities. Legally blind, she spent four hours each day crocheting caps for churches and Head Start programs to distribute to children. Her annual goal was a minimum of 150 caps. Her limited income did not stretch to cover yarn purchases, but friends and members of her church helped. "Many mornings I find a bag of yarn that somebody dropped off on my doorstep," she said.

Final Note: Tips for Being an Effective Volunteer

Once on the job, volunteers can increase their chances for productivity, skill-building, and enjoyable relationships with staff and coworkers by using the following tips.[9]

1. Attend training sessions and meetings.

2. Follow program policies and procedures.

3. Ask questions without hesitation when there is a problem or difficulty in understanding.

4. Keep open communications with the supervisor and coworkers. Be generous with appreciation and recognition of the positive aspects of the job. Approach problems with solutions and tact instead of blame.

5. Suggest improvements or changes in procedures by offering specific alternatives to the present ones, but do not take it as a personal affront if the suggestions are not followed.

6. With the supervisor, discuss personal goals for skill building so they can be coordinated with program goals. For example, a volunteer who wishes to gain writing skills could do so by working on press releases, organizational brochures, minutes of meetings, or the agency's annual report.

Notes

1. Richard N. Bolles, *The New Quick Job-Hunting Map* (Berkeley: Ten Speed Press, 1985).
2. Ibid., 13
3. Ibid.
4. Ibid.
5. *Attitudes of Americans over 45 Years of Age on Volunteerism* (Washington, DC: American Association of Retired Persons, 1988).
6. Barbara Kantrowitz, "The New Volunteers," *Newsweek,* 10 July 1989, 36.
7. W. Sweet, "Retired Scientists Provide Valuable Volunteer Work," *Physics Today* 37 (July 1984): 67.
8. Kantrowitz, "New Volunteers," 36.
9. Some of this information is adapted from *Self-Help Guide to Volunteering,* published by Mile High United Way (refer to the description in the Booklets, Manuals, and Pamphlets section of Chapter 5) and from suggestions of volunteer coordinators.

Chapter 3

Working with Older Volunteers

The previous chapters were directed at older adults who are seeking volunteer opportunities. This chapter is intended to help staff members and directors who work with older volunteers inside organizations. The material is not intended to serve as a comprehensive guide to volunteer management. Rather, it is a collection of observations, guidelines, and tips gathered from experienced staff and elder volunteers. It addresses the following topics:

Recruiting Older Volunteers

Dos and Don'ts in Managing Older Volunteers

Four Keys to Successful Management of Older Volunteers

Additionally, Chapter 4 lists professional societies for volunteer directors. Printed and audiovisual resources for professionals are identified in the annotations of the entries of Chapters 5 and 6.

Recruiting Older Volunteers

There are two transition points in older adulthood when individuals are apt to seek rewarding, meaningful ways to structure time and channel their skills and energies. These are times when individuals are likely to be receptive to invitations for volunteer commitments. The first transition point is retirement; the second occurs around age 75.

Recruiting Adults Before or Shortly After Retirement

Some men and women prefer to make volunteer commitments before they retire, so they will have something to step into when they leave the structure of full-time employment. Others want a year or two to catch up on activities such as fishing, tennis, bridge playing, home maintenance, and travel before they are ready to dedicate a portion of their time and energy to serving others. Many of the suggestions under "Recruiting Older Retired Adults" apply to this group. Additionally, the following can be helpful to the recruiter:

- Speaking with the human-resource staff or the person in charge of planning preretirement programs at local industries and businesses. Offering to present a brief explanation of volunteer opportunities at preretirement workshops or to provide printed information for workshop packets.

- Sending speakers, preferably volunteers, to give presentations at company-sponsored gatherings of retired employees. AARP suggests that an organization's "best 'advertisement' is the volunteer job description, accompanied by a brochure or other easy-to-read flyer identifying your organization and its goals."[1]

- Offering to write short articles on volunteer opportunities for retired employees' newsletters. This could be another assignment for a volunteer.

Recruiting Older Retired Adults

Three-and-a-half million Americans over age 75 continue to serve others through formal and informal volunteer work. For many of these adults, diminished energy, the onset of physical limitations, loss of a spouse, or boredom with current activities serve as a catalyst for either becoming volunteers for the first time or changing to a new area of volunteer work.

An example is Gertrude Casey, who after her retirement at age 64 became a self-taught guide and resource for points of interest in her city. She volunteered her services in schools and nursing homes and worked for pay as well. As she grew older, however, her severe arthritis necessitated hip and knee surgeries. A mild case of glaucoma dimmed her vision. At age 77 she began to learn storytelling and enrolled in training to become a peer counselor. Her new skills enabled her to continue volunteering despite her physical limitations.

Because individuals at this stage of life may be less mobile than younger persons, it is useful to consider creative methods of transportation and ways of involving them in service activities they can accomplish at home or in customary gathering places. For example, telephone calling, data entry and other computer work, mailings, and telephone reassurance work are all appropriate either for individuals to do at home or for group projects.

Nonprofit organizations frequently enlist the help of volunteers at senior centers in preparing mailings. In many communities, older adults participate in telephone reassurance programs for "latchkey" children. A former police radio dispatcher started reading to latchkey children after school. Spellbound by her husky voice, they invited their friends, and soon she had an enthusiastic following.

These are some additional ways to reach this pool of potential volunteers. The emphasis is both on helping volunteers get to the jobs and on taking the jobs to them.

- Arranging for articles featuring the work of volunteers in the local newspaper.

- Giving presentations on volunteer opportunities at residences for older adults. Often the board of resident representatives will assist by making time on a business-meeting agenda.

- Posting notices at senior citizens' centers.

- Contacting older-adults' groups at churches and synagogues. According to AARP, 28 percent of the volunteers over age 45 were recruited through their church.

- Contacting the staff and posting notices at senior citizen health clinics.

- Scheduling appearances by staff and volunteers on radio and television interview programs for older adults.

- Arranging carpools in which volunteers who drive pick up those who do not.

- Working with local public-transportation officials to arrange charter buses for groups of volunteers.

- When senior residences have their own vans, the recruiter may suggest that they be used to transport residents to volunteer jobs.

- Using networking. The recruiter can ask staff and volunteers, especially those in their fifties and sixties, whether they have friends or relatives who might participate in volunteer work. Individuals who would not otherwise venture forth are often willing to involve themselves when they are asked by a relative or friend. The 1988 AARP survey found that 30 percent of the volunteers were recruited through a friend or family member.

Dos and Don'ts in Managing Older Volunteers

The advice in this section comes both from managers experienced in working with older volunteers and from volunteers who had satisfactory or unsatisfactory experiences with their staff supervisors. People working with or managing older volunteers should:

1. Expect the same level of accountability from the older volunteer as from those of other ages.

2. Respect that adults learn in different ways and that learning styles are not dictated by chronological age.

3. Operate within the freedom there is. Explore ways to use a volunteer's abilities instead of placing undue emphasis on limitations or handicaps.

4. Be aware that some older adults are interested in employment and that they can acquire transferable skills through volunteer work. Inform interested volunteers of potential paying jobs within the organization.

5. Remember that many older adults enjoy the company of younger people and vice versa. Volunteer service can provide opportunities for such contact.

6. Be prepared for an intelligent, energetic volunteer when an older adult takes on an assignment. Keeping active is an often-mentioned reason for engaging in volunteer work by those over age 65.

7. Expect to see men as well as women take on volunteer work.

8. Understand that volunteers are busy and that most of them fit their service work into crowded schedules.

9. Consider older adults when dependability, conscientiousness, and long-term service are needed. At National Public Radio headquarters, several elder volunteers have been on the job for nine years. An 80-year-old volunteer for the federal Foster Grandparent Program recently received a prestigious award for outstanding service from a local television station. Each morning for four hours she fed, bathed, and held the babies in the intensive-care nursery of an urban general hospital. In 18 years on the job, she missed only four days.

Dangerous Assumptions

The most essential "don't" in managing older volunteers is "don't assume." Many of the popular myths about the aging process are based on partial truths, obsolete information, or the experiences of certain segments of the population. Older adults are so diverse that it is safe to say that their only common denominator is chronological age. When managing older volunteers:

1. Do not assume that retired persons want to do the same kind of work as volunteers that they did in their employment careers. A school principal might want to turn to carpentry. A researcher may have a yen to produce radio programs.

2. Do not assume that a handicap is as limiting to one person as it might be to another. For example, a hip fracture can permanently rule out stair climbing for one person. Another person may be able to resume normal activities after several months of recuperation.

3. Do not assume that older persons have difficulties with hearing or vision. On the other hand, the supervisor should be aware that impairments can be present and should check with each individual.

4. Do not assume that an older man or woman wants to be addressed by first name or last name. If there is any doubt, the supervisor should ask first. Most people appreciate the consideration and will want to fit in with the way others in the organization address each other.

5. Do not assume that older volunteers cannot or will not change. In every age group, some individuals accept change more willingly and graciously than others.

6. Do not assume that older volunteers want minimal responsibility. Some are prepared to take on major projects.

7. Do not assume that volunteers who stand back are unwilling to offer assistance and opinions. Many wait to be asked because they are not assertive, because they are unsure about their roles, or simply because they do not picture themselves as having opinions or being capable of certain activities until someone else introduces the possibility.

Four Keys to Successful Management of Older Volunteers

This section addresses four elements of sound volunteer management as they apply to older volunteers. It is a compilation of suggestions and examples from professionals experienced in managing older volunteers and from volunteers themselves. It is by no means a complete guide to managing volunteers. Instead, it is a set of tips for drawing upon the unique potential that older adults bring to their volunteer jobs. The references for this chapter cite a few of the excellent comprehensive guides to volunteer management.

Key #1: Matching Volunteers and Jobs

Following these steps will help ensure a good match between a job assignment and a volunteer's skills, interests, and expectations.

1. Use effective interview techniques

   In *The Effective Management of Volunteer Programs,*[2] Marlene Wilson explains the value of asking nondirective questions to elicit information. A nondirective question to gather information about preferred skills might be "What have you most enjoyed in previous paid and volunteer jobs?" Contrast the information-gathering potential of that question with this more directive approach: "What kind of work have you done in your previous jobs and volunteer positions?"

   Wilson emphasizes that job design and interviewing are essential "because without either of them, making good placements becomes a matter of sheer luck. . . . It is like fitting two parts of a puzzle together. When it is the right fit, it helps complete the whole picture of your organization."[3] The volunteer's resources of time, experience, and skills must be matched with the right job requirements and satisfactions in order to achieve a successful volunteer assignment. The interview process is crucial to this purpose.

2. Determine which skills the potential volunteer prefers to use

Some applicants for volunteer jobs are enthusiastic about using skills they acquired and polished in the past. They find them challenging and have no desire to switch but only to transplant them to new settings.

For instance, John Carson, who worked in the railroad industry for 45 years as a mechanic and inspector, was not ready to set aside his fascination with trains when he retired. He found opportunities to use his skills to restore the 100-year-old narrow-gauge trains of the Cumbres & Toltec Scenic Railroad in New Mexico and to help develop a railroad museum in his community.

By contrast, 71-year-old Katherine Sohnfeld reported that when she retired from 39 years of administrative work in government-land sales she was "ready for people contact and no more office work." As a volunteer, she matched elderly clients in need of assistance with volunteers of all ages who provided shopping, companionship, and other needed supports.

"It's tempting to pressure the person into taking a certain job in the agency when there is an urgent need and the volunteer's skills fit," observed Pat Brown, a former Red Cross volunteer coordinator. "But in the long run, it will work better for everyone if the staff listens to what the volunteer wants to do and makes assignments from there."

3. Determine which level of responsibility the volunteer wants

The supervisor should not make assumptions based on knowledge of the individual's past. A person recently retired from a demanding and highly responsible position might not want to immediately step into a volunteer leadership role. On the other hand, the challenge of leadership might be made-to-order for the volunteer who held a fairly routine paid job.

4. Inquire about the potential volunteer's expectations of the job

Understanding the individual's expectations not only makes it easier to match the volunteer with the job, but helps prevent future disappointment. The following are typical of the expectations that mature adults hold for their service involvements:

Chance to help others

Opportunity to stay active

Being around other people

Productive use of time

Chance to be needed

Avenue to learning new skills

Leads for employment opportunities

New experiences and challenges

Repay debt of gratitude to community or individual

Exposure to new viewpoints

5. Involve volunteers in selecting or designing their jobs

Char Halford, director of a victim/witness assistance program in a county district attorney's office, asked applicants to describe their long-range goals as volunteers and what they expect to derive from their jobs. She reviewed these with the applicants and explained to what extent the goals could be met through different jobs in the program. She gave examples of other volunteers' experiences and discussed time frames for meeting goals and expectations. She encouraged applicants to talk with other volunteers and to spend time observing the various operations in the agency before making job choices.

In some programs volunteers can create their own jobs by exploring what needs to be done and collaborating with others in formulating job descriptions. Sometimes volunteers are remarkably effective at designing jobs that improve program efficiency and effectiveness because they are free of preconceived notions about how things should be done.

6. Be flexible in creating volunteer jobs to match skills

If a volunteer offers skills and experience that do not readily match current openings, the manager should consider the possibility of expanding the program or service to use those skills. One example of this involved a husband and wife in Des Moines, Iowa, who wanted to work with handicapped children. Exploratory conversations with a special-education teacher resulted in a field trip on which a group of handicapped students visited the couple's orchard. The children rode the tractor, learned how the trees were tended, and picked apples that they took back to their school. The next day the couple came to the school and helped the children prepare and cook the apples. Then staff, volunteers, and students discussed the process of raising crops for food as they ate. From that beginning the couple became a regular adjunct to the school's program.

7. Use trial periods

As a backup to careful interviewing, a mutually acceptable trial period in a volunteer job can protect both volunteer and staff against an unsuccessful placement. In some programs this is a feasible choice; in others it is not. Directors who use trial periods agree unanimously that the volunteer and staff should maintain close communication during the trial period.

Key #2: Developing Useful Job Descriptions

The following are tips to consider in developing job descriptions for older volunteers.

1. Each volunteer job should have a title that is descriptive of the duties, sounds interesting, and is brief. "It helps in recruiting to have appealing job titles," said Katie Taylor, the volunteer coordinator for a ballet company. "Volunteers talk with their friends about their work. When they can explain their jobs in interesting terms, it gives a good image of your organization. That can also help in recruiting new volunteers."

2. Job descriptions for older volunteers should not be different than those for other age groups.

3. It should be mentioned in the job description whether reimbursement is available for out-of-pocket expenses such as parking, lunches, and bus fare.

4. The job description should specifically indicate the degree of flexibility in starting and finishing times for a job assignment. Volunteers who get rides or use public transportation need to know whether being early or late is acceptable.

Key #3: Designing Effective Training

As with job descriptions, training is an integral part of most volunteer programs. The following comments and observations will be helpful in designing effective training programs for older volunteers.

1. "Be sensitive to the differences in each person's learning style," advised Lavonna Kindle, director of a peer counseling program. "Some individuals learn well by role playing. Others are embarrassed by it. They learn better from printed instructions and trying things on their own."

2. Involve volunteers in designing their training experiences, especially after they have been on the job for a while. They have firsthand understanding of their learning needs.

3. When vision and hearing problems are present, adequate lighting, appropriate sound equipment, and well-produced printed matter are necessities. Many older adults welcome short standing and sitting times with frequent breaks for stretching.

4. Plan short training sessions with time for review. One volunteer stated her preference for this arrangement. "I like to see my job description first. Then I like to learn my job a little at a time. Getting everything at once is troublesome. I forget half of it, and it gives me the impression that my supervisor just wants me to get going so I can get out of her way."

5. Use a variety of training methods. They can include presentations, small group discussions, one-to-one sessions, audiovisual materials, role play, question-and-answer sessions, and related workshops and lectures outside the agency.

6. Help volunteers refresh their memories by providing plenty of opportunities for discussion and printed materials for review.

7. Time for socializing should be woven into training events. This adds to the enjoyment of the experience. Recall that the most-cited reason for volunteer participation, according to a 1988 American Association of Retired Persons survey, is personal enjoyment.

8. Give experienced, successful volunteers opportunities to train other volunteers. This is an acknowledgment of the former's achievements, and it provides a role model for other volunteers.

9. Include explanations of staff jobs in the training. This helps volunteers understand how they fit into the big picture. Further, it helps prevent misunderstandings. Taylor explained how she learned this the hard way. "One day our Data Entry Assistant arrived, and one of our staff stopped

his work at the computer so the assistant could start hers. Later I overheard her say that our staff person went into the other room and drank coffee while she worked. Our assistant had never been told about the other projects this employee worked on while she used the computer."

10. Training should be ongoing. A 72-year-old Senior Companion Program volunteer said, "I feel appreciated when we have a lecture or some training at our meetings. I've been in the program for three years, but I never want to stop learning how to do my job better."

11. Use training to give volunteers opportunities to grow in their jobs and to change jobs if they should so desire. "Sometimes they want just the minimum amount of responsibility when they start," said Halford. "Before long they decide that they're ready for more. Training allows them to make those moves. Volunteer directors should keep in mind that volunteers are susceptible to burnout just as employees are. If volunteers get burned-out on one job, we offer training in other aspects of our program. That way we don't lose them."

Key #4: Providing Meaningful Volunteer Recognition

Taylor makes a simple, eloquent case for treating volunteer recognition as an integral part of agency management: "Most nonprofit agencies simply could not provide their services without their volunteers." Volunteers and staff agree that recognition must be regular and frequent to be most effective. The informal, everyday expressions of appreciation carry at least as much weight as formal recognition events.

1. "Volunteers should be asked to take part in the planning of recognition events," Taylor suggested. She learned the value of this when she and several other paid staff planned a formal sit-down dinner with speeches and an award for their Volunteer of the Year.

Halfway through the preparations they discovered that the volunteer slated for the award disliked formal, sit-down gatherings. Recognition events that are compatible with the personalities and preferences of the honored guests are the most meaningful. Some individuals are embarrassed by public recognition, although others thrive on it. For some, personal letters are the most treasured appreciations.

2. Informal acknowledgments might include the following:

Birthday cards.

Get-well cards.

Verbal expressions of concern and support when a member of a volunteer's family is ill.

Thank-you notes for help through a particularly demanding project.

Inviting volunteers to participate in staff meetings.

Spontaneous compliments such as "Jane, it's such a pleasure to work with someone who is as prompt and reliable as you are," or "Hal, I overheard you handling Mrs. B's complaint—what skill and patience you have," or "Helen, thank you for all the effort you put into making the treasurer's report complete and accurate. I know our notes are not the easiest to decode."

3. In *Volunteer Recruiting and Retention: A Marketing Approach,*[4] Nancy Macduff suggested that volunteer-award policies be broad enough to include a diversity of service activities. This spreads the recognition around among volunteers. Recognition policies should be flexible enough to allow for change and growth in volunteer involvement as the program evolves.

4. Macduff further noted that criteria for formal volunteer awards should be thoughtfully planned and written into the agency's manual of operations.

5. Halford invites volunteers to staff meetings and staff training events. She views this as a form of volunteer recognition, as well as a vehicle for communication, training, and team building.

6. Including volunteers in decision-making is a form of recognition. A volunteer at a Denver, Colorado, food bank observed, "When my supervisor and other paid staff ask my opinion about changes and plans for the office, I feel appreciated. Even if changes don't directly affect my job, they will affect me in some way because I'm part of the team here."

7. Taylor noted that volunteers often prefer to have recognition events scheduled during their regular service hours. This is an important consideration when busy schedules, hesitance to venture out in the evening, or transportation difficulties are involved.

8. Organizations should take every opportunity to nominate outstanding volunteers for recognition outside the agency: for awards from the media, religious groups, business groups, and other community and national groups.

"A solid volunteer-recognition program contributes to a volunteer's job satisfaction," said Taylor. "Satisfied volunteers are goodwill ambassadors for your agency. Remember, they are great recruiters, too."

Notes

1. *Older Volunteers A Valuable Resource: A Guide for the Public and Private Sectors* (Washington, DC: American Association of Retired Persons, 1986), 13; order no. PF 3289(1086) D12025.
2. Marlene Wilson, *Effective Management of Volunteer Programs* (1976; Boulder, CO: Volunteer Management Associates, 8th printing, 1983), 125.
3. Ibid., 131.
4. Nancy Macduff, *Volunteer Recruiting and Retention: A Marketing Approach* (Walla Walla, WA: Macduff/Bunt Associates, 1985).

PART
TWO

Resources

Chapter 4

Directory of Organizations

Direct-Service Organizations

This is a highly selective compilation of organizations, associations, government agencies, and self-help groups whose work is related to volunteerism. They provide direct service to the public and enlist the help of volunteers in their work. Unless otherwise noted, they involve volunteers of all ages in their programs. When the organizations have local chapters, it is noted, so they can be contacted as quickly and easily as possible.

The goal in compiling this list was to provide the reader with the fullest possible understanding of the wealth of opportunities for rewarding volunteer work and to make it as easy as possible to obtain information. By no means is this an exhaustive directory of all the organizations in each field of concern. To locate complete guides to volunteer work in certain fields, please refer to the Directories section of Chapter 5.

Al-Anon Family Groups
Al-Anon Family Group Headquarters, Inc.
P.O. Box 862
Midtown Station
New York, NY 10018-0862
(212) 302-7240
(800) 356-9996

This is a self-help fellowship of relatives and friends of alcoholics who believe their lives have been affected by someone else's drinking. The Al-Anon recovery program is based on the Twelve Steps of Alcoholics Anonymous (AA). The identity of all Al-Anon and AA members is anonymous. Al-Anon's single purpose is to help families and friends of alcoholics, whether or not the alcoholic is still drinking. This worldwide fellowship of more than 30,000 groups in 100 countries came into existence in 1951. Volunteer opportunities exist in the organizational tasks and the person-to-person activities of a member-run support group. Membership is free of charge. Al-Anon is self-supporting through member contributions. It is not affiliated with AA, although the groups cooperate with one another. It is run by its members, not by professionals. Local groups are frequently listed in the phone directory. A state-by-state listing of groups is available from the headquarters office.

PUBLICATIONS: Numerous books and pamphlets on the effects of alcoholism.

Alcoholics Anonymous (AA)
General Service Board of Alcoholics Anonymous, Inc.
P.O. Box 459
Grand Central Station
New York, NY 10163
(212) 686-1100

AA is a voluntary, worldwide fellowship of men and women from all walks of life who meet together to attain and maintain sobriety. It is the pioneer of the self-help movement. There are no membership dues or fees. AA is supported only through member contributions. It is estimated that there are more than 76,000 groups with more than 1,500,000 members in 114 countries. AA members have many opportunities to volunteer in the work of coordinating local groups and participating in mutual member-support activities. AA is not operated by professionals. The anonymity of all members is protected. Groups meet in virtually every community. Check the phone directory for listings.

PUBLICATIONS: AA has an extensive publications program. It includes printed and audiovisual materials as well as posters and braille versions of some offerings. The costs are nominal.

Alzheimer's Disease and Related Disorders Association, Inc. (ADRDA)
Edward F. Truschke, President

70 East Lake Street, Suite 600
Chicago, IL 60601
(312) 853-3060
(800) 621-0379; (800) 572-6037 in Illinois

"Someone To Stand by You" is the motto of ADRDA, also known as the Alzheimer's Association. The organization is dedicated to research for the prevention, cure, and treatment of Alzheimer's disease and related disorders. It provides support and assistance to Alzheimer's victims and their families. ADRDA carries out its mission through five program areas: (1) research, (2) educational programs for the general public and health-care professionals on Alzheimer's and other forms of dementia, (3) local chapter formation to form a nationwide family-support network and to conduct programs in local communities, (4) advocacy for improved public policy and legislation to aid both victims of the disease and their care givers, and (5) patient- and family-service programs to assist present and future victims and their care givers.

PUBLICATIONS: ADRDA has an extensive publications program, including a quarterly newsletter that publishes research information, news of chapter activities, volunteer profiles, and resource information. Fact sheets and pamphlets provide factual information on Alzheimer's and related diseases, as well as information for family and care givers.

American Association of Retired Persons (AARP)
Horace B. Deets, Executive Director
National Office
1909 K Street, NW
Washington, DC 20049
(202) 872-4700

Dr. Ethel Percy Andrus founded AARP in 1958 on the motto, "To Serve, Not To Be Served." The association has four goals: (1) to enhance the quality of life for older persons; (2) to promote independence, dignity, and purpose for older persons; (3) to lead in determining the role and place of older persons in society; and (4) to improve the image of aging. With more than 400,000 volunteers, AARP is now the largest private, nonprofit, nonpartisan

membership organization in the world. The organization strives
to accomplish its four goals through programs and services that
enhance the quality of life for its members: by supplying information in the form of publications, television, and audiovisual
programs; through service opportunities that enable members
to improve others' lives and enrich their own; by taking action in
community service, legislation, research, communication, and
education to make a difference in the lives of all older persons;
and by providing member services in the form of financial,
insurance, and travel benefits.

AARP members may participate in a wide array of volunteer
services. These are the primary categories of service opportunities:

1. The Volunteer Talent Bank (VTB) is a computerized
   volunteer-to-position referral project designed to
   provide AARP members, and others who are age 50
   or older, with appropriate volunteer opportunities.
   Upon request, referrals may be made from the VTB
   central database of potential volunteers to AARP
   programs and activities, as well as to other
   organizations that meet AARP's participant
   guidelines. Volunteer applicants provide background
   on their interests, skills, talents, and availability.
   This data is used to match them with positions in
   programs and organizations. Volunteers are under
   no obligation to accept referrals.

2. Through the Citizen Representation program AARP
   volunteers advocate for legislative action and public
   policies that benefit older adults. Volunteers act as
   consumer representatives and members of advisory
   and regulatory boards. They conduct voter-
   education activities as well.

3. Volunteers in AARP's Criminal Justice Services
   address the needs of older persons for security in
   their living arrangements and protection against
   elder abuse. Criminal Justice volunteers serve
   law-enforcement agencies by doing tasks in police
   departments, and they provide mediation services in
   community programs.

4. Health Advocacy volunteers help older persons understand and obtain their Medicare/Medicaid benefits through organized programs in their communities. Additionally, these volunteers sponsor wellness fairs and screening programs in their communities.

5. The Housing volunteer program is concerned with helping older adults find appropriate housing and helping them to remain in their homes by modifying the dwellings to meet their needs.

6. Through Intergenerational Activities, AARP volunteers develop and support programs that enable old and young persons to build relationships that mutually enrich their lives.

7. Interreligious Liaison Volunteer Consultants work with groups of all faiths on programs for and with older persons. They help church and synagogue organizations implement innovative community volunteer programs.

8. Through the Personal Financial Security program, volunteers provide education, advocacy, and direct services to help persons over age 45 achieve financial security. The educational materials cover taxes, investing, and Social Security.

9. Reminiscence volunteers work with isolated elderly who are homebound or confined to nursing homes or retirement facilities. Their work gives individuals opportunities to see the meaning in their own lives and often recaptures historical information that is of broad community interest.

10. Tax-Aides give free tax counseling in cooperation with the U.S. Internal Revenue Service. Primarily they serve low- and moderate-income older persons. Tax-Aide is AARP's largest volunteer program with more than 8,500 sites nationwide in senior citizens' centers, churches, synagogues, libraries, and shopping malls.

11. Transportation volunteers work for the mobility of older persons through research, advocacy, and educational/public awareness efforts. Notable among their services is 55 Alive/Mature Driving, the nation's first driver-retraining program designed for older motorists. It is offered in communities throughout the United States. These volunteers also work on the mobility needs of the older nondriver.

12. Widowed Persons Service helps women and men recover from the loss of a spouse. In more than 200 locations, widowed volunteers give one-to-one support, make referrals, offer telephone reassurance, and conduct meetings to help ease the pain of loss. (A more detailed explanation of this volunteer effort may be found under the listing "Widowed Persons Service" in this section.)

13. Through AARP's Worker Equity Department, volunteers work with employers and older persons to implement programs that ensure employment opportunities, adequate retirement-planning opportunities, and promote understanding of the age-discrimination and pension laws.

To learn more about these volunteer opportunities contact a local AARP representative or one of the AARP Area Offices listed below.

Area I (Connecticut, Maine, Massachusetts, New Hampshire, Rhode Island, Vermont)
31 Saint James Avenue
Park Square Building
Boston, MA 02116
(617) 426-1185

Area II (Delaware, New Jersey, New York)
919 Third Avenue, Twenty-eighth Floor
New York, NY 10022
(212) 758-1411

Pennsylvania Inquiries:
Pennsylvania State Office
225 Market Street, Suite 502
Harrisburg, PA 17101
(717) 238-2277

Area III (District of Columbia, Kentucky, Maryland, North Carolina, Virginia, West Virginia)
1680 Duke Street, Second Floor
Alexandria, VA 22314
(703) 739-9220

Area IV (Alabama, Georgia, Mississippi, Puerto Rico, South Carolina, Tennessee, U.S. Virgin Islands)
Cambridge Building
2965 Flowers Road South, Suite 233
Atlanta, GA 30341
(404) 458-1491

Area V (Illinois, Indiana, Michigan, Ohio, Wisconsin)
2720 Des Plaines Avenue, Suite 113
Des Plaines, IL 60018
(312) 298-2852

Area VI (Iowa, Kansas, Minnesota, Missouri, Nebraska, North Dakota, South Dakota)
1901 West Forty-seventh Place, Suite 104
Westwood, KS 66205
(913) 831-6000

Area VII (Arkansas, Louisiana, New Mexico, Oklahoma, Texas)
8144 Walnut Hill Lane, Suite 700 LB-39
Dallas, TX 75231
(214) 361-3060

Area VIII (Colorado, Montana, Utah, Wyoming)
709 Kearns Building
136 South Main Street
Salt Lake City, UT 84101
(801) 328-0691

Area IX (Arizona, California, Hawaii, Nevada)
4201 Long Beach Boulevard, Suite 422
Long Beach, CA 90807
(213) 427-9611

Nevada Volunteer Office
c/o Jayne Wallace, Associate Area Representative (Area IX)
Howard Cannon Senior Services Center
340 North Eleventh Street
Las Vegas, NV 89101
(702) 386-8661

Area X (Alaska, Idaho, Oregon, Washington)
9750 Third Avenue, NE, Suite 400
Seattle, WA 98115
(206) 526-7918

PUBLICATIONS: AARP's publications program is extensive. It includes dozens of high-quality pamphlets, brochures, and booklets. The organization also produces many audiocassettes, films, and videocassettes. There are how-to materials for volunteers in each of the 13 service areas described above. Other materials address specific topics involving health, well-being, finances, and insurance for older adults and their families. A third category of publications explains AARP's member benefits. Of primary interest to volunteers is *Highlights,* the bimonthly newsletter that reports on AARP volunteer activities throughout the United States. *Modern Maturity* is AARP's official publication for members, featuring diverse subjects of interest to adults aged 50 and over. It would not be an overstatement to say that AARP publishes information on virtually any topic that is of interest to older adults and their families. AARP publications are available either at no charge or a nominal cost. Send to the National Office for the catalog *AARP Publications & A/V Programs: The Complete Collection* (PS0362(1288) C48) for a complete listing and ordering information.

American Cancer Society (ACS)
G. Robert Gadberry, Executive Vice-President
1599 Clifton Road, NE
Atlanta, GA 30329
(404) 320-3333

The ACS was established in 1913. Its activities are divided into the areas of education, research, and service. Educational activities are aimed toward the lay public and professional care givers. Service programs are implemented through volunteers who give support to cancer victims and their families. Volunteers are involved at every level—telephone work, clerical assistance, transportation of cancer patients for doctors' appointments, speakers bureaus, smoking clinics, publicity, and committee and board work. Each state and almost every metropolitan area has an ACS chapter. Check the American Cancer Society listing in the telephone directory for local-chapter information.

PUBLICATIONS: The ACS publications program is extensive. There are cancer prevention and detection materials for the general public, journals for clinicians, and training materials for volunteers. Audiovisual materials are available as well.

American Heart Association (AHA)
Dudley H. Hafner, Executive Vice-President
National Center
7320 Greenville Avenue
Dallas, TX 75231-4599
(214) 373-6300

AHA is dedicated to the reduction of premature death and disability from cardiovascular diseases and stroke. It has 55 state affiliates as well as county chapters throughout the United States. Since its founding in 1924, AHA has led the battle against heart problems on several fronts: education of the public about the effects of life-style on cardiovascular health; cardiovascular research; publication of literature for the general public on diet and exercise for healthy hearts; publication of research data; professional-education programs and materials; and patient-education materials for the physicians, nurses, and health-care professionals who care for heart patients. Volunteers work in all phases of the AHA's programs. They provide clerical support for ongoing programs and fund-raisers. Leadership positions are available on the boards of directors from the local to national levels. Service on program committees involves work with restaurants, schools, employers, speakers bureaus, and special educational events. The annual fund-raising drive requires the help of many volunteers in every community for onetime tasks or for year-round involvement. For information about AHA volunteer opportunities, check the telephone directory for a local American Heart Association listing.

PUBLICATIONS: AHA's publications program includes a large array of pamphlets, brochures, booklets, journals, and flyers for lay and professional audiences. Examples for lay audiences are "How To Make Your Heart Last a Lifetime," "Facts about Stroke," and "The American Heart Association Diet." Examples for professional audiences are *Circulation Research* (monthly) and *Cardio-Vascular Nursing* (bimonthly). For complete information on the publications contact the local AHA office or the National Center.

American Hiking Society Volunteer Vacations (AHS)
Susan Henley, Executive Director
P.O. Box 86
North Scituate, MA 02060
(703) 385-3252

Volunteer vacations are demanding, yet so rewarding that each year more than one-third of AHS volunteers are alumni. AHS has projects at 29 sites throughout the 50 states. Examples include trail rehabilitation in the Grand Canyon, trail construction in Alaska's Chugach National Forest, campsite maintenance in the Massachusetts Boston Harbor Island State Park, and exotic-plant control on top of a volcano in Hawaii's Haleakala National Park. The vacations usually last one to two weeks with relaxation and sightseeing time included. Good physical condition, camping equipment, familiarity with backpacking, and transportation and registration costs are all required. Volunteer vacation expenses are tax deductible.

PUBLICATIONS: Among the publications of AHS are *Helping Out in the Outdoors: A Directory of Volunteer Work and Internships on America's Public Lands,* published semiannually. A two-year subscription is $12; single copies are $3 each.

American Red Cross (ARC)
Gil Tills, Senior Vice-President and Chief Operating Officer
National Headquarters
Seventeenth and D Streets, NW
Washington, DC 20006
(202) 737-8300

The ARC has a 125-year history as a private, nonprofit service organization. Its services include the maintenance of blood banks, relief to disaster victims, training programs in cardiopulmonary resuscitation, first aid, and water safety. Red Cross nurses and volunteers conduct health-education efforts and screening and immunization clinics throughout the United States. The military and their families receive Red Cross communications assistance. Through the International Committee of the Red Cross, the League of Red Cross, and Red Crescent Societies, Americans receive help in contacting family members in other parts of the world when disaster strikes. ARC uses the services of 1.4 million volunteers in the United States. These men and women work in disaster situations, collect and distribute blood, drive Red Cross vehicles, visit the elderly, teach community-service courses in health maintenance and accident prevention, and perform a myriad of other services, depending on the needs of the community. Training is provided for all volunteer jobs. Nearly every community has at least one Red Cross program. Check the telephone directory under American Red Cross for a local listing.

PUBLICATIONS: The ARC publications program is vast. It includes numerous educational materials on all of ARC's service areas. Contact the local chapter for details. *Volunteer 2000 Study* is a five-volume document completed in 1988 that contains the history of volunteerism in the ARC, issues in volunteerism and volunteer administration confronting the ARC now and in the future, statistical findings of the study, and recommendations emerging from this massive study of volunteerism and related issues within the ARC.

Association for Living Historical Farms and Agricultural Museums, Inc.
(ALHFAM)
Smithsonian Institution
National Museum of American History, Room 5035
Washington, DC 20560

> This is the central, international service organization for those
> involved in living historical farms, agricultural museums, and
> outdoor museums of history and folk life. ALHFAM was founded
> in 1970 as a vehicle for communication among individuals and
> organizations interested in agricultural and rural history. The
> annual meeting serves as a forum for exchanging ideas, informa-
> tion, experience, and skill. The association provides standards
> and guidance for managing and operating living historical farms
> and related facilities, whether staffed by professionals or volun-
> teers. ALHFAM has regional organizations in the United States
> and Canada.
>
> PUBLICATIONS: ALHFAM publishes the *Bulletin,* which gives
> members a bimonthly update on activities, training opportuni-
> ties, and annual-meeting plans. It has bibliographies, book re-
> views, articles, and classified ads. *Proceedings,* compiled from
> each annual meeting, contains papers and workshop summaries
> from the presentations of specialists in the field. It is a useful
> reference piece. The *Replica Source List,* available to members
> upon request, provides a listing of individuals and companies
> who deal in products useful in living history settings.

Citizen Action
Ira Arlook, President
P.O. Box 33304
Washington, DC 20033-0304
(202) 857-5168

> "Issues of the '90's" is Citizen Action's agenda for the decade. It
> consists of "making health care accessible and affordable; pro-
> tecting communities against toxic wastes and the pollutants that
> contribute to Global Warming; controlling utility rates; breaking
> up the auto-insurance stranglehold; grappling with corporate
> merger-mania and the decline in well-paying jobs; [and] address-
> ing the plight of families, the poor, and family farmers." Citizen
> Action conducts public hearings, demonstrations, lobbying visits,
> petition drives, and "accountability sessions" where constituents

meet with elected officials. Volunteer opportunities with the organization are voter education through canvassing, volunteer recruitment, issues development and writing briefing papers, staffing telephone banks, working with the news media, and general office work. Internships with Citizen Action are available in the Washington, D.C., office on a volunteer basis. Interns develop analytical, verbal, and writing skills in the making of federal and state public policy. They gain experience in research, congressional advocacy, and grass-roots organizing. Applicants should submit a resume and letter of introduction to the Internship Coordinator at the Washington, D.C., office. Citizen Action has affiliates and allies in California, Connecticut, Florida, Idaho, Illinois, Indiana, Iowa, Maine, Maryland, Massachusetts, Michigan, Minnesota, Missouri, New Hampshire, New Jersey, New York, North Carolina, Ohio, Oregon, Pennsylvania, Texas, Washington, West Virginia, and Wisconsin.

PUBLICATIONS: *Citizen Action,* the quarterly newsletter, covers developments on the organization's issues. Other publications are educational brochures for members and the general public.

Common Cause
Fred Wertheimer, President
2030 M Street, NW
Washington, DC 20036
(202) 833-1200

Common Cause is a nonpartisan citizens' lobbying organization founded in 1970 by John Gardner, former Secretary of Health, Education, and Welfare. With more than 280,000 members nationwide, Common Cause works for reform issues it deems as high priority. Current priorities are congressional campaign-finance reform, nuclear-arms control, tax reform, and ethics and accountability in government. Through a combination of professional lobbying efforts and write-in and call-in campaigns by members in the 50 states, the organization calls congressional attention to priority issues. Volunteers at the Washington, D.C., headquarters act as liaisons to activists at state and local levels. Other volunteer work includes monitoring congressional hearings, answering mail inquiries, working with the staff of *Common Cause Magazine,* administrative duties, handling public relations, and doing research for publications. Regional and local volunteers do many of the same kinds of jobs as well as organizing write-in and call-in campaigns when issues come before the Congress.

PUBLICATIONS: The organization's official publication is *Common Cause Magazine,* an award-winning bimonthly journal of investigative articles, short news items, and editorials on the organization's priority issues. It is sent to all members.

Earthwatch
Brian A. Rosborough, President
680 Mount Auburn Street
P.O. Box 403
Watertown, MA 02172
(617) 926-8200

Earthwatch was founded in 1971 to serve as a bridge between the public and scientific communities. Each year the organization sponsors more than 100 expeditions around the world. Paying volunteers join researchers and scholars for two to four weeks to work on projects in the following areas: art and archaeology, geosciences, life sciences, marine studies, and social sciences. Volunteers are of all ages; 29 percent are over age 56. Many come for "repeat performances." The record is held by a 78 year-old woman who has joined 23 expeditions. Earthwatch provides training for its volunteers. The brochure states, "We're looking for people who want to help and learn. No special skills are required. We teach you everything you need to know to help in the field." Volunteer opportunities are open exclusively to Earthwatch members.

PUBLICATIONS: The membership magazine, *Earthwatch,* is published seven times each year and features articles about the organization's projects and findings. Members also receive the annual *Explorer's Guide and Diary.*

Foster Grandparent Program (FGP)
ACTION
Jane Kenny, Director
1100 Vermont Avenue, NW
Washington, DC 20525
(202) 634-9349

ACTION, the federal government's volunteer agency, sponsors FGP. It is open to low-income men and women age 60 and over. Volunteers work with physically and mentally handicapped children in projects throughout the United States. Since its founding in 1965, FGP volunteers have served children in hospitals and institutions. Today pilot projects are underway to meet the needs of abused and neglected children in their own homes. Through their presence on a regular weekly schedule, Foster Grandparents bring caring and stability to the lives of their foster grandchildren. Volunteers receive a modest, tax-free stipend, a transportation allowance, hot meals while in service, accident insurance, and annual physical examinations. Orientation consists of 20 to 40 hours of pre-service training followed by monthly in-service training sessions. Contact the central office for information about local projects.

Friends of the Cumbres & Toltec Scenic Railroad, Inc. (FCTSR)
Dan Ranger, General Manager
P.O. Box 789
Chama, NM 87520
(505) 756-2151

FCTSR's objective is to preserve railroad history in New Mexico and Colorado, particularly as it relates to the Cumbres & Toltec Scenic Railroad. This 64-mile stretch of narrow-gauge track runs through the mountains between Antonito, Colorado, and Chama, New Mexico. It was built in 1880. The steam-powered train, originally used in mining operations, now serves as a vehicle from which hundreds of passengers can view the spectacular mountain scenery. It operates from the summer season through autumn. The railroad is jointly owned by the states of Colorado and New Mexico. It is a Registered National Historic Site, operated under a contract with Kyle Railways of San Francisco, California. Volunteers gather each summer at specified times to work on maintenance, restoration, and enhancement projects involving the train, the tracks, and the depots at Chama and Antonito. Fund-raising activities throughout the year provide revenue for equipment and materials. Volunteers with all types of skills are welcome to help since the work is highly diversified. Needed skills range from the mechanical to the artistic, and from clerical to journalistic. Volunteers are urged to apply at least six months in advance for the maintenance projects as openings are limited.

Global Volunteers
Burnham J. Philbrook, President
2000 American National Bank Building
St. Paul, MN 55101
(612) 228-9751

>   Global Volunteers is a not-for-profit corporation whose mission is to promote international understanding and peace. The volunteer program centers around two-week personal learning and work experiences in rural, developing communities. The men and women who participate share their skills with others, while gaining a new perspective of the world. They help village residents with projects that will improve their lives, such as planning schools, construction, tutoring, and agricultural programs. Project sites include communities in Tanzania, Jamaica, India, the Philippines, Western Samoa, and Mexico. All backgrounds, ages, and occupations find useful involvement in Global Volunteers' work: teachers, mechanics, lawyers, actresses, nurses, carpenters, managers, homemakers, students, farmers, physicians, computer operators, artists, chemists, and others. Volunteer training includes predeparture seminars on the culture, history, economics, politics, and climate of the area, practical dos and don'ts, packing, team-building, basic language training, and health concerns. Returned volunteers participate in training new ones. Volunteers pay their own way. All trip-related costs are tax deductible. Trips range from 16 to 21 days and cost roughly $1,100 to $3,000. Global Volunteers has membership categories for organizations, families, individuals, and students.
>
>   PUBLICATIONS: Global Volunteers' official publication is *Communique,* a newsletter for members and volunteers.

Gray Panthers
Frances Humphreys, Director
311 South Juniper Street
Philadelphia, PA 19107
(215) 545-6555

1424 Sixteenth Street, NW
Washington, DC 20036
(202) 387-3111

>   Maggie Kuhn and five friends founded the Gray Panthers in 1970. Their goal, then and now, is to see that the abundance of

the United States be shared by all its citizens. Presently there are more than 80 local chapters with membership totaling 70,000. Through political action, volunteers work to assure that the young and old have adequate housing and health care. At the local level, Gray Panther networks endeavor to preserve rent control and to prevent evictions of people over age 65 when buildings become condominiums. They promote housing in which young and old live under the same roof. In some areas they have helped to change local zoning laws to allow shared living for nonrelated persons. This often prevents homelessness.

PUBLICATIONS: *Gray Panther Network: Age and Youth in Action* is a bimonthly newspaper of articles written by well-respected authors on topics such as environmental concerns, economics, and political policy. Editorials and news of local Gray Panther programs appear in each issue.

Hospice Education Institute (HEI)
M. J. M. Galazka, Executive Director
Five Essex Square
P.O. Box 713
Essex, CT 06426
(203) 767-1620
(800) 331-1620

HEI has three areas of service: it helps individuals find hospice care; it advises community leaders, health-care planners, and civic organizations on issues related to hospice care; and it works with educators who teach courses on dying, grief, and bereavement. HEI conducts regional seminars and workshops on various aspects of hospice care for qualified hospice volunteers and health and caring professionals. HOSPICELINK maintains a computerized and frequently updated directory of hospices in the United States. The information is available to the public at no charge. HOSPICELINK offers general information about the principles and practice of hospice care and helps those who wish to start hospices in their hometowns. Persons who would like to become hospice volunteers can use HOSPICELINK to locate programs in their communities. HEI was established in 1985.

International Executive Service Corps (IESC)
Thomas S. Carroll, President

Eight Stamford Forum
P.O. Box 10005
Stamford, CT 06904-2005
(203) 967-6000

IESC recruits retired executives and technical advisors in the United States to share their years of experience with businesses in developing nations. Retired U.S. executives work side by side with entrepreneurs of small and medium-sized enterprises in developing countries. By providing managerial know-how and up-to-date business techniques, IESC's "shirtsleeve ambassadors" help emerging businesses create new jobs, produce new products and services, and absorb local labor and raw materials. They provide assistance and develop guidelines that clients can use to become self-sustaining. IESC has answered requests to help businesses of all kinds: from producers of handbags to steel-mill industries. When assistance is requested, IESC recruits from a Skills Bank of 10,000 men and women who have agreed to volunteer their services. Project assignments last from a few weeks to a year. Spouses accompany volunteers and work on service projects in the host community. IESC pays travel and living expenses for volunteers and their spouses. IESC's major emphasis is on development of a host country's private enterprise. Founded in 1964, the organization is partially sponsored by the Agency for International Development and a large number of U.S. corporations.

PUBLICATIONS: *IESC News*, a newsletter published six times a year, covers news items from projects that are underway and lists current IESC project assignments.

Laubach Literacy Action (LLA)
Peter A. Waite, Executive Director
1320 Jamesville Avenue
P.O. Box 131
Syracuse, NY 13210
(315) 422-9121

LLA's purpose is to enable adult native speakers of English and speakers of other languages to acquire basic-level skills in listening, speaking, reading, writing, and mathematics and to help these persons solve problems encountered in their daily lives, enabling them to participate more fully in their communities. LLA accomplishes its purpose by creating learning partnerships between adults who want to learn and volunteers who want to teach. The organization works through a national network of adult-literacy programs that engage trained volunteers as tutors. It acts as a national resource center for individuals and organizations seeking information on the issue of illiteracy. LLA cooperates with agencies and institutions in training volunteers for the tasks of promoting literacy. These tasks include individual tutoring, assessing community needs and resources, volunteer recruitment and training, developing partnerships with other organizations, and program evaluation. LLA serves more than 750 communities in 45 states. Its parent organization is Laubach Literacy International, which conducts reading programs abroad. Both organizations build on the work of Dr. Frank C. Laubach, whose philosophy was that literacy is a fundamental tool in the struggle for individual dignity and social justice. He founded LLA in 1968.

PUBLICATIONS: LLA's publications include a constantly growing selection of training materials. *The Laubach Literacy Action Directory* lists literacy programs and individual trainers. For a complete description of this publication, please see the summary in the Directories section of Chapter 5.

League of Women Voters of the United States (LWV)
Grant P. Thompson, Executive Director
1730 M Street, NW
Washington, DC 20036
(202) 429-1965

The league promotes political responsibility through informed and active participation of citizens in government. It takes concerted action to secure public policies consistent with the league's positions. The league has 1,245 local leagues. It is open to citizens, male or female, age 18 or over. LWV volunteers participate in voter-registration drives, assist in organizing polling places on election days, develop publications on local and national public-policy issues, and arrange for public forums wherein political candidates air their views. Since its establishment in the 1920s, the LWV has advocated for such matters as child-care programs, voting rights, the ERA, and nuclear-arms control.

PUBLICATIONS: The LWV membership magazine, *National Voter,* is available to nonmembers for a subscription fee. It features in-depth coverage of timely national issues that are on the league's agenda, news of grass-roots action, and national lobbying activities. The League Action Service (LAS) consists of the periodic newsletter *Report from the Hill.* "Action Alerts," also part of LAS, notifies subscribers about issues when their letters or telephone calls will have the greatest impact on their congressional representatives. The *LWV Catalog,* updated annually, offers guides to understanding the political process and promoting citizen participation in the local community.

Lions Clubs International
Mark Lukas, Executive Administrator
300 Twenty-second Street
Oak Brook, IL 60570-0001
(312) 571-5466

The Lions were founded in Chicago, Illinois by a group of businessmen in 1917. Although the Lions are best known as a men's service organization whose primary focus is on sight conservation, both the membership and mission have expanded since their founding. In 1987, women were extended full-membership privileges on an international basis. The Lions' extensive sight-conservation work includes the establishment of glaucoma detection centers, eye-research foundations, eye banks, training facilities for guide dogs, and rehabilitation centers. In addition to sight conservation, Lions are involved in a drug-education effort called "Skills for Adolescence." It is aimed toward junior-high and middle-school students. The organization also conducts diabetes awareness and research programs that offer general screenings and services for diabetic children. There are more than 39,000 Lions Clubs worldwide. The members assist with fundraising projects for Lions' programs and participate in local community-service projects.

PUBLICATIONS: The official publication is *The Lion,* published ten times a year. The magazine carries news of Lions' activities throughout the world and human-interest features on members and recipients of Lions' services. A brochure describing the slide, videotape, and film presentations on Lions' programs is available free of charge.

Literacy Volunteers of America (LVA)
Jinx Crouch, President
5795 Widewaters Parkway
Syracuse, NY 13214-1846
(315) 445-8000

> LVA provides a range of services that enable people to achieve their personal goals through literacy. LVA gives tutoring and other educational services directly to individuals who aspire toward increased literacy skills. The organization also helps those who are learning English as a second language. In addition to its direct literacy services to clients, LVA trains volunteers to become tutors. LVA is as committed to the success of its volunteers as it is to the clients it serves. This commitment is explicit in the mission statement: "Through training and support, we help build the skills and abilities that enable volunteers to grow and succeed." Volunteers participate in basic reading and conversational English workshops. A variety of video, slide, and tape presentations combined with print materials support and extend the basic training. LVA offers technical assistance and training materials to support the organization and management of literacy programs nationwide. Frequently LVA works in conjunction with local and national groups, such as B. Dalton Bookseller, libraries, state departments of education, and the U.S. departments of education and labor. The organization has 240 local groups. Contact the headquarters office for information about local activities.
>
> PUBLICATIONS: LVA publishes a wide array of guides, how-to manuals, tapes, and slide/tape presentations on various aspects of promoting literacy. Here are a few examples: *Tutor: Techniques Used in the Teaching of Reading, Management Handbook for Volunteer Programs,* and *Telephone Tutoring Module.* A complete catalog is available upon request.

March of Dimes Birth Defects Foundation
Charles L. Massey, President
1275 Mamaroneck Avenue
White Plains, NY 10605
(914) 428-7100

The March of Dimes started in 1938 as the leader in the battle against polio. Since the late 1950s, it has dedicated its efforts to preventing and treating birth defects. The organization conducts research on the genetic causes of birth defects as well as those causes related to the mother's life-style. Through its public-education programs, the March of Dimes teaches women the basics of prenatal health. Through its professional education programs, health professionals enhance their skills in the care and treatment of babies with birth defects. Recently, the March of Dimes has channeled many research and treatment resources into the problems of children born to drug-addicted mothers. The organization has local chapters whose volunteers work on fund-raising, educational programs, and screenings.

PUBLICATIONS: Educational materials for public and professional audiences.

Mothers Against Drunk Driving (MADD)
Micky Sadoff, President
669 Airport Freeway, Suite 310
Hurst, TX 76053
(817) 268-6233

After Cari Lightner, age 13, was killed by a hit-and-run drunk driver, her mother started MADD. Since its founding in 1980, MADD has grown to a nonprofit corporation with more than 400 chapters in the United States, Canada, New Zealand, and Great Britain. Its mission statement is "In a nation where an average of 23,500 people are killed annually by drunk drivers, the challenge to solve this crisis and end these senseless tragedies forms the core of MADD's objectives." The organization has been instrumental in the enactment of drunk-driving laws, establishing victims' and survivors' rights programs, and educational programs about drunk driving. MADD volunteers conduct youth-education programs about safe driving, and youth training in the techniques of avoiding dangerous situations involving alcohol and drug use. Speakers bureaus offer trained speakers to address civic and professional organizations on traffic-safety issues, victims rights, community action, and prevention techniques to remove intoxicated drivers from the highways. Hundreds of concerned citizens attend MADD workshops annually.

The organization has led the movement for greater attention to victims' and survivors' rights in the courts. For information on the judicial process and support groups, there is a victim hotline, (800) 438-MADD (6233).

PUBLICATIONS: The *MADD Student Library* contains statistics, case studies, ideas for student activities, and a bibliography of resources on highway-safety issues. Other publications include booklets for victims of drunk-driving crashes, techniques for avoiding drunk driving, and information for supporting and comforting victims and survivors of drunk-driving crashes. The newsletter, *MADD in Action,* is published bimonthly, and *MADD-vocate,* a magazine for victims and their advocates, comes out quarterly.

National Arbor Day Foundation (NADF)
John Rosenow, Executive Director
100 Arbor Avenue
Nebraska City, NE 68410
(402) 474-5655

NADF is an educational organization whose work is made possible by more than 800,000 members and supporters. The five programs include (1) Conservation Trees, a multimedia communications project on planting, managing, and saving trees for their conservation value; (2) Tree City USA, which provides direction, technical assistance, and public recognition for urban and community forestry programs; (3) Trees for America, through which NADF distributes millions of trees and publishes educational materials that help citizens improve their tree planting and care techniques; (4) Celebrate Arbor Day! "recognizes the good stewards of today and educates the good stewards of tomorrow through celebrations in communities across the United States"; (5) J. Sterling Morton Orchard and Tree Farm, in Nebraska City, Nebraska, is a National Historic Landmark and center for education and research on conservation. Morton commemorated the first Arbor Day more than 100 years ago. Among NADF's supporters are individual citizens, public officials, public agencies, schools, and volunteer organizations. Its programs are implemented in cooperation with, and through, groups in local communities.

PUBLICATIONS: NADF is known for its authoritative and visually splendid publications. They include the bimonthly magazine *Arbor Day,* which carries news of conservation activities as well as educational articles. NADF produces a large selection of educational materials for use in schools and community programs.

National Association for the Preservation and Perpetuation of Storytelling (NAPPS)

Jimmy Neil Smith, Executive Director
P.O. Box 309
Jonesborough, TN 37659
(615) 753-2171

NAPPS was founded in 1975 at the conclusion of the third National Storytelling Festival in Jonesborough. The nonprofit organization is "dedicated to encouraging a greater appreciation, understanding, and practice of storytelling." It has members in each state and several foreign countries. NAPPS serves as a resource for groups and individuals who want to know more about the storytelling art, its meaning and importance, and its uses and applications in modern life. NAPPS fulfills its mission through two major activities. First, it conducts the National Storytelling Institute, a summerlong program of storytelling education for persons of all backgrounds. Participants learn to use storytelling in the workplace and as volunteers in community programs. Second, NAPPS sponsors the annual National Storytelling Festival in Jonesborough. Here dozens of tellers and thousands of listeners gather to be entertained and educated by the art of storytelling. Membership in NAPPS allows reduced admission fees to its events, access to group-health insurance, free subscriptions to several publications, access to the NAPPS library and archives, and technical assistance at no charge.

PUBLICATIONS: NAPPS publishes the *National Catalog of Storytelling,* the quarterly *National Storytelling Journal,* and the monthly newsletter *The Yarnspinner.* NAPPS also publishes and updates the *National Directory of Storytelling* with U.S. and foreign listings of storytellers, storytelling organizations and centers, festivals, conferences, schools, educational events, and newsletters.

National Association of Partners in Education, Inc. (NAPE)
Daniel W. Merenda, Executive Director
601 Wythe Street, Suite 200
Alexandria, VA 22314
(703) 836-4880
(800) 992-6787 (For publications orders
with purchase orders or credit cards only)

> Since 1964 NAPE has provided assistance and support to schools in the use of volunteer services and to community volunteers who enhance classroom instruction. The organization is currently directing attention toward the effective use of elder volunteers as mentors, tutors, and guest speakers as well as assistants in classrooms and school libraries. NAPE has 10,000 members. NAPE's National School Volunteers Program (NSVP) accepts individual memberships. Membership benefits include volunteer liability insurance, a subscription to the quarterly volunteer newsletter, and discounts on conference registrations. Members are eligible for national-recognition awards.

> PUBLICATIONS: NAPE publications include a monthly newsletter, *Partners in Education*. It features national news of interest to association members and information about local projects. The publication's catalog lists NAPE's manuals, research summaries, and audiovisual aids. Materials are available to individual volunteers who wish to build and enhance their skills, to program administrators, and to classroom teachers.

National Association of Retired Federal Employees (NARFE)
H. T. Steve Morrissey, President
1533 New Hampshire Avenue, NW
Washington, DC 20036-1279
(202) 234-0832

> NARFE is comprised of 500,000 federal civilian retirees, current federal civilian employees with five years vested service, and their spouses and survivors. It has 1,700 chapters in the United States, Puerto Rico, Guam, the U.S. Virgin Islands, Panama, and the Philippines. Its objectives are twofold: to protect the fiscal concerns of federal retirees and to encourage members to work for the good of their local communities either through NARFE

chapters or through other means. In 1985 NARFE joined with the Alzheimer's Disease and Related Disorders Association (ADRDA) to sponsor a massive fund-raising effort to support research on the disease and to ease the burden on families of Alzheimer's victims. Local NARFE chapters conduct fund-raising events and public-awareness campaigns regarding Alzheimer's.

PUBLICATIONS: NARFE publishes the booklet "National Program To Conquer Alzheimer's Disease," which outlines procedures for local-chapter participation in the joint effort with ADRDA. *Retirement Life* is NARFE's monthly membership magazine. Other bulletins and newsletters disseminate information on the organization's special programs.

National Association of Volunteers in Criminal Justice (NAVCJ)
William F. Winter, Executive Director
c/o University of Wisconsin-Milwaukee Criminal Justice
P.O. Box 786
Milwaukee, WI 53201
(414) 229-5630

NAVCJ is a membership association whose goal is to increase citizen involvement in the justice system. It was founded in 1970. Membership is open to all individuals and organizations interested in improving juvenile and criminal justice through citizen initiative. NAVCJ seeks to enhance the image of justice volunteerism by serving as an advocate for citizen volunteers, developing relationships with organizations having similar goals, and building the efforts of local programs across the United States and Canada into an international constituency. There are 11 regional groups in the United States and Canada. Current membership stands at 400. Members have access to workshops, networking opportunities, and an annual training forum featuring noted speakers. The quarterly newsletter, use of the NAVCJ library, and discounts on all literature purchases are additional benefits of membership.

PUBLICATIONS: *NAVCJ In Action,* the newsletter that keeps members informed of justice volunteer activities throughout the United States and Canada, is published quarterly. NAVCJ also publishes research reports, monographs, and training materials.

National Center for Mediation Education (NCME)
2083 West Street, Suite Three-F
Annapolis, MD 21401
(301) 261-8445

> NCME is a nonprofit educational organization. Its goal is to change the way family conflicts are resolved. It provides alternatives to the adversarial legal process by encouraging family-mediation research, by training mediators, and through public education. NCME provides an international referral service to family mediators. Eventually, this service will make referrals to qualified mediators in other areas of conflict resolution. Consulting services are available from NCME. Training programs include a basic 40-hour family-mediation program and advanced training. Other offerings are lectures and one-day introductory programs for professionals and the general public.
>
> PUBLICATIONS: *Starting Your Own Mediation Practice: A Workbook* and other training materials are available through NCME.

National Coalition for the Homeless (NCH)
Mary Ellen Hombs, Director
1621 Connecticut Avenue, NW, Fourth Floor
Washington, DC 20009
(202) 265-2371

105 East Twenty-second Street
New York, NY 10010
(212) 460-8110

> Founded in 1982, NCH is a federation of individuals, agencies, and organizations who are committed to the principle that decent shelter, housing, and adequate food are fundamental rights of a civilized society. The coalition serves as a clearinghouse to share information and other resources. It offers legal assistance to local groups representing the rights of the homeless. It teaches groups and individuals how to take political action on behalf of the homeless. It produces detailed annual reports on homelessness in targeted cities or states in an effort to increase public awareness of the issue and to spur action. NCH refers interested persons to community projects that are engaged in helping the homeless. To reach the National Volunteer Hotline, operated by the Community for Creative Non-Violence, call (800) 435-7664.

PUBLICATIONS: NCH publishes many reports on homelessness in metropolitan and rural areas, on legislation relating to homelessness, and information on other problems that surround homelessness. The newsletter, *Safety Network,* is published in two versions each month: one by the office in New York and the other by the Washington, D.C. office.

National Committee for Prevention of Child Abuse (NCPCA)
Anne H. Cohn, D.P.H., Executive Director
332 South Michigan Avenue, Suite 1600
Chicago, IL 60604-4357
(312) 663-3520

NCPCA has a nationwide network of child-abuse-prevention organizations with volunteers in each state. These volunteers design and implement programs to meet local needs. There are parenting-education classes, family life skills classes, and support groups for new parents. Instructional programs for children teach self-protection against abuse. In hundreds of communities there are treatment programs for abuse victims. Some programs provide family visitors who give respite and support to parents; others advocate against corporal punishment in schools and child-care programs. NCPCA also sponsors training for professionals and volunteers. These prepare the attendees to implement community programs and to engage in strategies for continued efforts to prevent child abuse.

PUBLICATIONS: NCPCA makes available materials for parents, children, teachers, medical professionals, and prevention/treatment specialists. Some of the educational materials are available in Spanish.

National Council of Catholic Women (NCCW)
Annette P. Kane, Executive Administrator
1275 K Street, NW, Suite 975
Washington, DC 20005
(202) 638-6050

The NCCW is a federation of Catholic women's organizations in the United States. It provides a network for the more than 8,000 women's groups in 118 dioceses whose membership totals in the millions. It has been active since 1920. The network enables Catholic women to address and take action on contemporary problems. NCCW members serve on private and public policy-making bodies monitoring a variety of social justice issues. NCCW's committees include Church Communities, Family Affairs, International Affairs, Community Affairs, Organization Services, and Legislative Information. The national headquarters provides its affiliate groups with information on current issues of interest to Catholic women, program materials for community action, and research data on which to build effective social programs. "Respite" is an NCCW-sponsored program with groups in communities throughout the country. It provides trained volunteers who stay with an elderly person for a short period of time so that the family can have time for other activities. This program is part of NCCW's emphasis on enabling the aged to live meaningfully within their families. NCCW assists local groups in establishing Respite programs and training the volunteers.

PUBLICATIONS: NCCW publications include *Catholic Woman*, the membership magazine issued six times a year. It features articles on programs and resolutions relevant to NCCW's work. The newsletter, *Colloquy*, is published three times a year. "Legislative Alerts" comes out as needed to prompt members to take action on specific pieces of legislation. Other publications include position papers on human rights, justice for women, aging, and women in the church; and a resource list, "Don't Face Alcohol & Drug Problems Alone." Training kits and resource packets are available for individuals as they assume offices and responsibilities in NCCW.

National Council of Jewish Women (NCJW)
Dadie Perlov, Executive Director
53 West Twenty-third Street
New York, NY 10010
(212) 645-4048

Founded in 1893, this is the oldest Jewish-women's volunteer organization in the United States. NCJW has more than 100,000 members in at least 200 sections across the country. The organization's purpose is to advance human welfare and the democratic way of life. The purpose is approached in three ways: social action, education, and community service. Today NCJW concentrates its efforts on children and youth, the aging, women's issues, Jewish life, constitutional rights, quality of life in Israel, and research. Volunteers may serve on local projects and in leadership positions at every level of the organization.

PUBLICATIONS: NCJW produces many brochures explaining the facets of its work. One brochure, for example, explains the group's national resolutions. Additionally, there are training manuals on initiating specific service programs, such as *How To Publish a Directory of Services for Older Adults* and *Continuing Choices: A Comprehensive Handbook of Programs for Work with Older Adults*. Because of their general applicability, these two publications are summarized in the Booklets, Manuals, and Pamphlets section of Chapter 5.

National Exchange Club Foundation for the Prevention of Child Abuse
James A. Schnoering, Secretary-Treasurer
3050 Central Avenue
Toledo, OH 43606-1757
(419) 535-3232

In 1979 The National Exchange Club (NEC) adopted child-abuse prevention as a national project. At that time NEC formed its Foundation for the Prevention of Child Abuse with its own board and trustees to fund and administer the project. The foundation operates a nationwide network of Exchange Club Centers for the Prevention of Child Abuse. Professionally trained volunteers from the centers work directly with abusive parents and their children in the families' own homes. In addition, the clubs sponsor seminars, distribute informational materials, and engage in other activities aimed toward the prevention of child abuse. The NEC is involved in other service projects, including crime prevention and youth programs. NEC regularly recognizes the "good deeds of heroes and heroines of everyday life and [documents] their accomplishments as an inspiration to future generations." The theme of NEC's work is "Americans serving America." It strives to promote appreciation of American citizenship and works to make the United States a better place to live. The organization has grown to more than 1,200 clubs in the United States and the Commonwealth of Puerto Rico since its beginning in 1911. In 1985 NEC opened membership to women.

National Friends of Public Broadcasting (NFPB)
Sally Ouweneel, Chairman
c/o WFYI–Channel 20
1401 North Meridian Street
Indianapolis, IN 46202
(317) 271-8404

> NFPB is a resource for local volunteer groups who are work-
> ing on behalf of public radio and television stations in local
> communities. It was founded in 1970 to give volunteers and paid
> staff opportunities to exchange ideas on developing community
> support and awareness of public broadcasting. NFPB's main
> activity is its annual conference. Here participants share ideas
> and experiences regarding fund-raising, volunteer recruitment,
> and increasing audiences for public broadcasting. Outstanding
> volunteers receive awards at the conference.

> PUBLICATIONS: NFPB's official publication is the newsletter,
> *Newsbreak*.

National Public Radio (NPR)
2025 M Street, NW
Washington, DC 20036
(202) 822-2000
(800) 235-1212

> NPR is a private, not-for-profit membership organization in-
> corporated in 1970. NPR's members are public-radio stations,
> which currently total more than 350. The member stations are
> in 48 states, Puerto Rico, and the District of Columbia. A distin-
> guishing feature of NPR and its member stations is the absence
> of advertisements. Funding for public radio comes from corpo-
> rate, foundation, and federal grants as well as private contri-
> butions. NPR works in partnership with member stations by
> producing in-depth news, features on social issues, human-interest
> shows, and performances of music, drama, and variety material,
> which member stations may use. The member stations, in turn,
> produce performance programs and often file news stories
> that NPR presents nationally. NPR's in-depth news programs,
> "Morning Edition" and "All Things Considered," are widely
> acclaimed. The NPR office in Washington, D.C. and the 350
> local public-radio stations use volunteer services extensively.

Because each station operates independently, volunteers work in different capacities at each one. According to Anne Kaufman, volunteer coordinator at the Washington, D.C., office, volunteers handle telephone requests for information, enter data into the computer, organize and conduct tours of the facilities, prepare mailings, coordinate the work of other volunteers, and paste up newspaper clippings. "Some of our volunteers have been with us for eight or nine years. We particularly like having mature adults because they are so dependable and they handle public inquiries so well." Other public-radio stations report that their volunteers do much of the telephone and clerical work connected with periodic fund-raising campaigns, conduct telephone surveys of members, work at station-sponsored concerts and other community activities, and sometimes get involved in producing and broadcasting programs.

PUBLICATIONS: "Member Stations," a state-by-state listing of public-radio stations. Each listing includes the station's call letters and position on the radio dial. This is available at no charge.

National Retiree Volunteer Center (NRVC)
Donna S. Anderson, President
905 Fourth Avenue South
Minneapolis, MN 55404
(612) 341-2689

"Retirees: America's untapped resource" is the motto of NRVC, founded in 1986. Through training and consultations to corporations and communities, NRVC enables retirees, with the support of their employers, to develop volunteer programs. The programs allow retirees to apply their career skills and expertise to community issues. Frequently, volunteers work within the established programs of nonprofit organizations. Their work reaches into such areas as literacy, drugs, education, youth-at-risk, hunger, the handicapped, older adults' services, arts, housing, health-care delivery, criminal justice, and child care. NRVC grew out of a project of the Junior League of Minneapolis, Minnesota. Presently more than 18 corporations with more than 4,000 retiree volunteers and 200 community agencies are involved. NRVC's five-year goal is to mobilize two million volunteers through 250 programs in 25 cities in the United States.

PUBLICATIONS: *NRVC Roundtable,* the membership newsletter.

Older Women's League (OWL)
Joan Kuriansky, Executive Director
730 Eleventh Street, NW, Suite 300
Washington, DC 20001
(202) 783-6686

OWL is an action-oriented organization committed to improving the lives of mid-life and older women. Since its founding in 1980, it has formed local chapters in more than half of the states. Seven key issues comprise OWL's national agenda: protecting and upgrading women's Social Security benefits; correcting inequities in public and private pensions as they affect women; affordable health care for all Americans; respite services to providers of in-home care for the chronically ill; combating age and sex discrimination in employment; redirecting national-budget priorities; and keeping end-of-life decisions in the hands of individuals. In local OWL chapters, volunteers educate their communities and policymakers about the unique concerns of mid-life and older women. Many of these concerns stem from women's longer life expectancy. OWL members develop mutual self-help and support networks on employment, housing options, economic, health, and legal issues. OWL helps older women become self-directed and action-oriented, since they are likely to survive their spouses by at least seven years. Contact OWL headquarters for information about local chapters.

PUBLICATIONS: OWL publishes *The OWL Observer,* a bimonthly newspaper that covers local chapter events, national OWL news, and legislative items regarding the organization's priority issues. OWL also publishes "Mother's Day Reports," Gray Papers, how-to packets, booklets, and videos on such topics as divorce and older women, living wills, durable powers of attorney, care-giving, planning in advance for health-care decisions at the end of life, and women and pensions.

Peace Corps
Loret M. Ruppe, Executive Director
1990 K Street, NW
Washington, DC 20526
(800) 424-8580

Peace Corps volunteers of all ages help people in developing countries become self-sufficient. They come by invitation from the country's leaders. Living among the citizens, volunteers work on food production, safe-water supplies, nutrition, health, education, and other vital needs. Their work results in upgraded knowledge and skill levels among the native population, economic development, better income and housing, more available energy, conservation of natural resources, and better community services. Older adults are especially welcome in the Peace Corps since many cultures value the experience and wisdom of elders. There is no upper age limit for volunteers, but basic legal and medical criteria must be met. Volunteers receive language, technical, and cross-cultural training. They receive particular attention to such personal needs as health care, support systems, living allowances, communication with family, and safety. Financial-readjustment allowances help volunteers reenter life in the United States after their assignments.

PUBLICATIONS: *Peace Corps in the 80's* is the twenty-fifth anniversary update on the Peace Corps' projects, accomplishments, and goals. *Peace Corps Times,* a bimonthly magazine, is a guide to successful transitions for returned volunteers. It carries articles on the process of making transitions and profiles of successfully readjusted volunteers, as well as job leads in the United States and abroad. The Peace Corps produces informative videos on its service opportunities. For selected descriptions, please see the Films and Videos section of Chapter 6.

Project VOTE!
Sanford A. Newman, Executive Director
1424 Sixteenth Street, NW, Suite 101
Washington, DC 20036
(202) 328-1500

As a nationwide, nonpartisan program, Project VOTE!'s objective is to promote voter registration and voter turnout among low-income and minority citizens. The organization trains minority and low-income organizers to help targeted citizen groups understand how elections affect them. Created in 1982, the organization pioneered the strategy of registering citizens to vote as they waited in lines to collect unemployment checks, food stamps, and social services. Volunteers for Project VOTE! receive intensive training and follow-up supervision. Training is implemented through a combination of group training sessions and videos. Three training videos with supplementary written materials are available for sale: "What's Your Last Name? The Five Steps of Voter Registration" demonstrates a five-step approach and additional tips for volunteers working on voter registration and petition drives. "Let It Shine: Motivating and Training Volunteers" teaches five keys to volunteer motivation. It uses the "Tell/Show/Do" training cycle. The material is applicable to all types of volunteers. It uses, as its example, teaching an organizer how to run a motivation and training session for registration volunteers. "How Am I Going To Recruit Them?" teaches the key elements of a volunteer recruitment pitch and the follow-up calls to make sure volunteers show up. The written materials for this video include tips and sample pitches for different settings, how to find volunteer leads, and problem solving in recruitment situations. Project VOTE! is a project of Americans for Civic Participation and the Project VOTE! Fund.

Retired Senior Volunteer Program (RSVP)
ACTION
Jane Kenny, Director
1100 Vermont Avenue, NW
Washington, DC 20525
(202) 634-9353

RSVP is a program of ACTION, the U.S. government's volunteer agency. Volunteers work in nonprofit private and public community organizations throughout the United States. They may either use skills from their professional careers or talents developed in an avocation, such as art or theater. The work ranges from direct involvement with the needy, homebound, elderly, or teenagers to behind-the-scenes services such as office work, carpentry, or staffing hotlines. Schedules are arranged by mutual agreement of the volunteer and agency staff. Four hours a week is a typical time commitment. RSVP welcomes anyone age 60 or older, retired or semiretired, with any level of education, experience, and income. RSVP staff provide a brief orientation, and staff at the volunteer site do in-depth instruction and supervision. Volunteers receive accident and liability insurance as well as incidental expenses such as transportation.

Salvation Army (SA)
National Headquarters
799 Bloomfield Avenue
Verona, NJ 07044
(201) 239-0606

Eastern Headquarters
120 West Fourteenth Street
New York, NY 10011

Central Headquarters
860 North Dearborn Street
Chicago, IL 60610

Southern Headquarters
1424 North East Expressway
Atlanta, GA 30329

Western Headquarters
30840 Hawthorne Boulevard
Rancho Palos Verdes, CA 90274

The SA is an international religious and charitable movement. Founded in 1865 in London, England, by William Booth, it came to the United States in 1880. It now has more than 10,000 U.S. centers. It is organized and operated in a quasi-military manner as a branch of the Christian church. Through employees and hundreds of volunteers, SA's work involves emergency lodges and "skid row" centers; dispensaries and clinics; general and maternity hospitals; counseling for unwed mothers; employment services; missing-persons bureaus; drop-in centers and military kits for the armed forces; services in correctional institutions; adult-rehabilitation centers; social-service centers; aid to victims of disaster; and Christmas kettles to raise funds for the needy.

PUBLICATIONS: The Salvation Army publishes *The War Cry,* its official biweekly publication, and *All the World,* a missionary magazine. SA has films for schools, churches, and community groups as well as other program materials.

Self-Help Clearinghouse (SHC)
Edward J. Madara, Director

St. Clares-Riverside Medical Center
Pocono Road
Denville, NJ 07834
(201) 625-9565

SHC helps individuals and organizations learn about, and make connections with, mutual aid self-help (MASH) groups. It distributes computer software and a database entitled MASHnet as aids to program development for other self-help clearinghouses. SHC sponsors the Mutual Aid Self-Help section on the national Compuserve computer-information service. Through the MASH Networking Project, SHC helps individuals with rare conditions to develop new national and international self-help networks.

PUBLICATIONS: An important aspect of SHC's service is its publications program. Among its materials are the *Directory of Self-Help Clearinghouses Worldwide* and *The Self-Help Sourcebook: A Comprehensive National Guide to Finding & Forming Mutual Aid Self-Help Groups.*

Senior Companion Program (SCP)
ACTION
Jane Kenny, Director
1100 Vermont Avenue, NW
Washington, DC 20525
(202) 634-9349

Senior Companions provide supportive services that often enable frail elders to remain in their own homes rather than moving to nursing homes. Companions help their clients by arranging services from community agencies, assisting with personal affairs, scheduling transportation, and easing the transition back home after a hospital stay. Often Companions extend friendship to alleviate loneliness or depression. The length of service to clients can vary from a few weeks to several years. Senior Companions are low-income men and women aged 60 and older. Committed to serving 20 hours each week, they typically divide their time among three clients. Schedules are flexible. The SCP provides a modest, tax-free stipend as well as accident and personal-liability insurance while on assignment, an allowance for transportation, and an annual physical examination. Companions receive 40 hours of pre-service orientation and four hours of in-service training every month. All 50 states have SCPs. Call or write for information about local programs.

Service Corps of Retired Executives (SCORE)
Active Corps Executives (ACE)
1129 Twentieth Street, NW, Suite 410
Washington, DC 20036
(202) 653-6279
(800) 368-5855

As volunteer programs of the U.S. Small Business Administration, SCORE and ACE provide counseling services to small businesses. SCORE volunteers are retired executives; ACE volunteers are still employed. Services are free of charge to small businesses and to would-be entrepreneurs. SCORE's 12,000 members work in their local communities. There are 400 offices in the United States, Puerto Rico, the Virgin Islands, and the trust territories of the Pacific. SCORE matches the needs of the client with the expertise and interest of the counselor. Some SCORE volunteers conduct seminars on different aspects of business from the planning through the implementation stages. Volunteers do a great deal of one-to-one counseling with business owners. This can last from one week to a year, depending on the needs of the business.

SHARE-USA
World SHARE, Inc.
Reverend Mr. Carl Shelton, President
3350 E Street
San Diego, CA 92102
(619) 525-2200

SHARE is an innovative combination of volunteerism and barter. The SHARE program purchases large quantities of food at wholesale prices and sells it at cost to people in local communities. Individuals purchase the food with a combination of cash or food stamps and volunteer service. The cash price is approximately one-third of the retail value. The service requirement is two hours of service for each bag of food. The volunteer service may consist of bagging or distributing food at the SHARE site. It may also be done in other community programs or on a one-to-one basis. While the food items vary each month, the bags always have fresh produce and meats, staples, and one or two processed items. New SHARE chapters are constantly forming in communities throughout the United States. In each state the chapter takes on the state's name, for instance, SHARE-New Jersey. Once the first site is formed in a state, others follow. World SHARE has divisions in Guatemala and Mexico.

PUBLICATIONS: A monthly newsletter that combines news about world, national, and local SHARE activities. It also features nutrition information and recipes using the foods in the current month's food bag.

Sierra Club
Michael L. Fischer, Executive Director
730 Polk Street
San Francisco, CA 94109
(415) 776-2211

This is a nonprofit public-interest organization of nearly one-half million members in 57 chapters. Sierra Club "promotes conservation of the natural environment by influencing public-policy decisions—legislative, administrative, legal, and electoral." Funds for the club's work come from memberships and contributions. John Muir became the club's first president when it was founded in 1892. Since then, Sierra Club has been involved in the following conservation efforts: creation of the National Park Service, creation of Glacier National Park, protection of the Clean Air Act, passage of the Water Pollution Control Act in 1972, and campaigns to protect the Arctic National Wildlife Refuge. Each year the Sierra Club designates an action agenda, for example, global warming and national-lands protection. The club engages in lobbying, expert testimony, grass-roots activism, and public education on conservation matters. Volunteers participate in every aspect of Sierra Club's activities. Each year the club sponsors outings for youth, the disabled, and older adults.

PUBLICATIONS: The Sierra Club publishes *Sierra,* an award-winning magazine that is sent to all members six times a year, and *National News Report,* a summary of environmental news, published about 26 times a year with a special emphasis on legislation. The club also has an extensive list of public-affairs booklets on such topics as environmental action, land use, energy, population, outdoor activities, and international environmental issues. Sierra Club has published more than 350 books; it produces an array of calendars and engagement books each year. It offers slide shows, videos, and filmstrips as well. All the Sierra Club chapters publish newsletters.

Society of St. Vincent de Paul (SVDP)
Council of the United States
Rita W. Porter, Executive Secretary
4140 Lindell Boulevard
St. Louis, MO 63108
(314) 371-4980

> The aim of the SVDP is "to bring social justice and the friendship of true charity to all those in need." The society is a worldwide lay organization of Catholics who work at the parish and district levels. Volunteers design their efforts to meet local needs and available resources; their work comes under the following classifications: services to those in poverty; information and referral; extending Christian faith, hope, and love to the lonely and forgotten; emergency services; promotion of social justice; and help for the elderly and handicapped. Current SVDP membership in the United States is more than 61,000.

> PUBLICATIONS: The society's publications include a monthly bulletin, "Vincenpaul," and the quarterly newsletter, *Ozanam News*.

Task Force on Families in Crisis (TFFC)
Mrs. Tottie Ellis, Executive Director
P.O. Box 120495
Nashville, TN 37212
(615) 383-4575

> This organization emerged from the public hearings of the United States Attorney General's Task Force on Family Violence in the mid-1980s. In 1986, TFFC was awarded a cooperative agreement with the Office for Victims of Crime within the U.S. Department of Justice. TFFC's goals are "to energize the private sector, including businesses, civic groups, churches and clubs, to prevent domestic violence, and to strengthen families." Through its public education program, TFFC distributes videos, sermon tapes, lecture tapes, recommended reading lists, information on programs for families and individuals, radio programs, materials

for religious workers, and a national directory of private services that aid victims and abusers. TFFC works with law-enforcement personnel and with legislators to help develop and enforce laws regarding family violence. Programs for violence prevention, victim protection, and counseling for batterers are developed at the local level. Through community task forces, TFFC encourages and enables local citizens and the private sector, including employers, to develop and implement plans for preventing spouse abuse. A centralized speakers' bureau has been established listing both national and local speakers. TFFC members conduct seminars, community forums, and programs in schools and churches. Volunteers for TFFC come from every walk of life and participate in all facets of the group's work.

PUBLICATIONS: TFFC has publications for families, law-enforcement officials, religious workers, program planners, employers, social workers, and abuse victims. The *Directory of Private Services* lists private services (not primarily funded through governmental sources) for victims, abusers, or any member of a family experiencing violence. Please refer to the Directories section of Chapter 5 for more information on TFFC's national directory.

Telephone Pioneers of America
William Jermain, Executive Director
Association Headquarters
22 Cortlandt Street
New York, NY 10007
(212) 393-3252

More than three-quarters of a million men and women are Telephone Pioneers. These are individuals who spent 17 or more years in the telephone industry. Some are retired; others are not. Pioneers contribute millions of hours to service projects, for which they raise approximately $10 million annually. The organization has 105 chapters in 12 regions spanning the United States and Canada. The Pioneers are known for their services to the blind. Particularly notable are their inventions that ease the problems of blindness. For example, the Pioneers invented the Beepball, a softball that allows the visually impaired to enjoy ball games. The Pioneers are the official repair designee for the U.S. Library of Congress' Talking Book program. Pioneers work on maintaining the Appalachian Trail, building and refitting parks and playgrounds for the disabled, and in campaigns against drunk driving. Each chapter has its own projects for rendering direct service and raising money to help with community needs.

PUBLICATIONS: *The Telephone Pioneer* is the quarterly newspaper for members.

United States Forest Service (USFS) Volunteers Program
P.O. Box 96090
Washington, DC 20090
(202) 535-0920

Volunteers are in increasing demand to help meet the escalating recreational use of public land. Volunteer job options are widely varied, offering both outdoor and indoor work. The Campground Host Program offers assignments in recreational areas for a few days to an entire season. Volunteers also serve as trailhead hosts, giving information to the public as well as keeping track of the departures and arrivals of hikers. Other volunteer work involves photography, computer operation, tour guidance, fire prevention, conducting educational programs, tool and equipment maintenance, and trail building and maintenance. In many USFS districts, the staff will work with volunteers to design job descriptions that meet local USFS needs. Among them might be creation of brochures, development of special tours, wildlife conservation, research, and equipment inventories. Although the greatest need for volunteers is during the summer, there are year-round opportunities for involvement. It is common for volunteers to come back for repeat assignments. One Kansas couple, for example, has chalked up ten summer assignments in the Colorado mountains and they plan to continue as long as they are able.

Volunteers often provide their own tents or trailers for lodging or stay with friends or relatives. USFS staff may also assist in locating living arrangements. Free camp sites and propane tanks are sometimes provided. Expenses are paid for some assignments. Volunteers are covered for on-the-job injuries. Contact the national headquarters or the local U.S. Department of Agriculture for application materials and information about regional USFS offices. Apply 6 to 12 months in advance for seasonal assignments.

Volunteers in Overseas Cooperative Assistance (VOCA)
Donald D. Cohen, President
50 F Street, NW, Suite 1075
Washington, DC 20001
(202) 626-8750

> Upon request from developing countries, VOCA sends volunteers to cooperatives, other private-sector agricultural enterprises, and government agencies. Through VOCA's Cooperative Assistance Program, volunteers help organize cooperatives, manage credit unions, improve agricultural production and farm management, help with food processing and storing methods, and work on marketing. The Farmer-to-Farmer Program matches experienced farmers from the United States with those in developing countries who are seeking to improve their farming operations. VOCA was founded in 1970 as a private nonprofit organization funded by the United States Agency for International Development. Volunteers' expenses are paid while on assignment, and they are provided with interpreters, work quarters, and secretarial help. Volunteers are typically retired or in mid-career with backgrounds in farming, cooperatives, or agribusiness. Overseas assignments range from 30 to 90 days. Couples sometimes work together on projects. VOCA recruits volunteers from its talent pool as requests for assistance are approved.

Volunteers in Service to America (VISTA)
ACTION
Jane Kenny, Executive Director
1100 Vermont Avenue, NW
Washington, DC 20525
(202) 634-9445

> VISTA is a full-time, yearlong volunteer program for men and women from all backgrounds. The volunteers work with persons of low income to help them become more self-sufficient. Local sponsors, to whom VISTA volunteers are assigned, may be state or local public agencies or private, nonprofit organizations. The program is active in the 50 states, the District of Columbia, Puerto Rico, and the Virgin Islands. Service projects can be located in urban or rural areas or on Indian reservations. Usually volunteers serve in or near their own communities. They extend

their skills and experience to concerns that include drug abuse, literacy, employment training, food distribution, shelter for the homeless, neighborhood revitalization, and needs of the elderly and prenatal care. All volunteers receive pre-service training through VISTA, and further training in any skills necessary for the assignments is conducted through the sponsoring agency. A monthly stipend is granted to defray expenses. Contact the national headquarters for information about regional VISTA offices.

Volunteers in Technical Assistance (VITA)
Henry R. Norman, President
1815 North Lynn Street, Suite 200
P.O. Box 12438
Arlington, VA 22209-8438
(703) 276-1800

VITA brings technical knowledge, skills, and experience to citizens in developing countries. Its volunteers design simple, inexpensive applications of advanced technologies to solve problems, and create social and economic opportunities. VITA is a nonprofit organization established in 1960 by scientists and engineers who wanted to share knowledge, skills, and experience with people in developing countries. Current VITA project priorities are small-enterprise development, renewable-energy applications, agriculture, reforestation, water supply and sanitation, and low-cost housing construction. Volunteers include craftspersons, engineers, technicians, agriculturalists, veterinarians, and others who teach the local citizens skills with which they can become self-reliant. Applicants for volunteer assignments complete the application materials. Their names are then placed in the skills bank for follow-up when projects develop through requests from host countries. Assignments vary from short- to long-term. Some volunteer-support work for the organization is available in the United States.

PUBLICATIONS: *VITA News* is a quarterly magazine that highlights development programs and trends. VITA Publications Services publishes a catalog each year offering dozens of how-to materials on small-scale, low-cost technology applications.

Volunteers of America (VOA)
Raymond C. Tremont, President

3813 North Causeway Boulevard
Metairie, LA 72220
(504) 837-3652
(800) 654-2297

> With offices in more than 200 communities in the United States, VOA offers programs for the elderly, families in distress, troubled youth, former offenders, persons with alcohol or drug dependencies, the mentally and physically disabled, the hungry, the homeless, and other groups with special needs. VOA is a Christian ministry founded in 1896. Its programs often grow out of partnerships with business and industry, affiliated agencies, and churches. It involves professional staff and volunteers in each of its widely varied programs. Contact the national headquarters or check the White Pages in the telephone directory for a local VOA office.

> PUBLICATIONS: *The Gazette,* VOA's national quarterly publication, highlights local program accomplishments and the contributions of volunteers and staff as well as news items.

Widowed Persons Service (WPS)
American Association of Retired Persons (AARP)
1909 K Street, NW
Washington, DC 20049
(202) 872-4700

> WPS serves widowed men and women of all ages, helping them cope with the adjustments to widowhood. WPS volunteers are widows. They receive extensive training that qualifies them to provide the following services: (1) outreach, visiting the newly bereaved and discussing their problems; (2) telephone services, offering telephone numbers the widowed can call for referral information and assistance; (3) group sessions at which widowed persons can discuss their problems and provide mutual assistance; (4) public education, using the resources of local public-service agencies and educational media to call attention to the needs of the widowed and the services available to them; and (5) referral services, providing widowed persons with a directory of local services. WPS has chapters in many local communities. They are often affiliated with AARP units as well as religious, educational, and social-service organizations. WPS programs are usually managed by volunteers instead of paid staff.

PUBLICATIONS: Among WPS publications is *On Being Alone: AARP Guide for Widowed Persons*. It covers such topics as coping with bereavement, family adjustment, employment, and financial and legal matters.

Young Men's Christian Association of the United States of America (YMCA)
Solon Cousins, Executive Director
101 North Wacker Drive
Chicago, IL 60606-7386
(312) 977-0031

The mission of the YMCA is "to put Christian principles into practice through programs that build healthy body, mind, and spirit for all." Since its founding in 1851, the YMCA has enacted its mission primarily through youth programs, including day camps, swimming, child care, and mentoring. In recent years it has expanded its concern to encompass both the homeless and frail older adults. The YMCA actively seeks volunteer involvement from older adults. Opportunities for meaningful volunteer jobs abound in the 2,050 YMCA branches throughout the United States. Currently there are more than 324,000 program volunteers serving 13 million people each year. More than 65,000 volunteers serve in policy-making positions on boards and task forces. Contact the local YMCA for information about volunteer work.

Young Women's Christian Association of the United States of America (YWCA)
Gwendolyn Calvert Baker, Executive Director
726 Broadway
New York, NY 10003
(212) 614-2700

The programs of the YWCA are diverse. They are tailored to address the needs of the 4,000 communities that have YWCA chapters. All activities support the organization's purpose: "to draw together into responsible membership women and girls of diverse experiences and faiths, that their lives may be open to new understanding and deeper relationships, and that together they may join in the struggle for peace and justice, freedom and dignity for all people." Typical YWCA services might include personal-growth classes, fitness programs, employment counseling, child-

care referral services, and speakers' bureaus, for example. Since
its founding in 1858, the YWCA has conducted international
programs at the invitation of host countries. Volunteer opportunities are available from the local to national levels. Volunteers
participate in leadership and policy-making and all other aspects
of the YWCA's programs. The local YWCA chapter should be
contacted for further information.

Professional Societies

This is a representative listing of professional societies whose
objectives include the promotion of volunteerism among older
adults. Many professional education and development programs
are offered by direct-service organizations as well. Where this is
so, it is noted in the program descriptions in the listing of direct-
service organizations.

American Society of Directors of Volunteer Services of the American
Hospital Association (ASDVS)
Nancy A. Brown, Director
840 North Lake Shore Drive
Chicago, IL 60611
(312) 280-6000

ASDVS's purposes are to develop the knowledge and compe-
tence of the individual member, to provide a means of intercom-
munication for directors of volunteer services and health-care
institutions, to conduct surveys, to provide consultation to vol-
unteer-services management, and to establish and maintain professional standards and ethics. To be eligible for ASDVS
membership, one must be responsible for volunteer services in
hospitals. The society provides its members with periodic survey
reports, the departmental-evaluation guide entitled "Assessment
of the Department of Volunteer Services in a Health Care Institution," and an ASDVS membership roster. There are currently
more than 50 local affiliates. Activities include an annual meeting and educational conference.

PUBLICATIONS: ASDVS publishes *Hospitals,* the biweekly journal of the American Hospital Association, which carries news
and features of interest to hospital administrators and managers.

Volunteer Services Administration, the ASDVS quarterly news-letter, carries information and progress reports on the society's activities, projects, and programs.

Association for Volunteer Administration (AVA)
David Tobin, Executive Director
P.O. Box 4584
Boulder, CO 80306
(303) 497-0238

> The mission of AVA is to promote and strengthen the profession of volunteer-services management. The organization has 12 regions that provide leadership, educational career development, networking, and collaborative opportunities. AVA sponsors the only professional certification program in the field of volunteer management. It was established 1967. Educational endorsement is offered by AVA for workshops and courses that meet the standards of the association. Members may attend regional and national conferences. Membership in AVA is open to both salaried and nonsalaried persons active in volunteerism and vol-unteer-services administration.

> PUBLICATIONS: The AVA publishes *The Journal of Volunteer Administration,* a quarterly featuring articles on practical con-cerns in the field, philosophical issues, and significant research. *Update* is AVA's bimonthly newsletter. *Professional Ethics in Volunteer Services* is a guide to professional ethics and stan-dards for volunteer administrators. *Current Issues Update* is a bimonthly report on issues relating to volunteerism.

The Foundation Center
Thomas R. Buckman, President
79 Fifth Avenue
New York, NY 10003
(212) 620-4230
(800) 424-9836

> The Foundation Center is a resource and service provider to professionals in nonprofit organizations. It publishes a broad range of material on private, community, and corporate founda-tions. Grant makers and grant seekers will find the services particularly valuable. The center disseminates information on

foundation and corporate giving through library collections at the following locations:

79 Fifth Avenue
New York, NY 10003
(212) 620-4230

1001 Connecticut Avenue, NW, Suite 938
Washington, DC 20036
(202) 331-1400

At both facilities, reference librarians will assist patrons in locating materials. The center has also a network of 175 cooperating libraries in all 50 states and abroad that maintain substantial collections of materials related to volunteerism. Films and videos are available from the Foundation Center on a purchase or rental basis. Computer users will find the organizations's databases helpful resources on grants available and application guidelines. For details on the center's databases, please refer to the Foundation Center listing in the Electronic Media section of Chapter 6. The Foundation Center maintains field offices at

312 Sutter Street
San Francisco, CA 94108

Hanna Building
1422 Euclid Avenue
Cleveland, OH 44115
(216) 861-1933

PUBLICATIONS: The center's publication program is extensive and diverse. Recent books include *National Guide to Funding in Aging* and a career guide for the nonprofit world, *Careers for Dreamers and Doers*. A catalog lists all of the Foundation Center's publications, audiovisual materials, and computerized services. Address written inquiries to Department LC at the New York headquarters.

Generations Together (GT)
Sally Newman, Executive Director
University of Pittsburgh
811 William Pitt Union
Pittsburgh, PA 15260
(412) 648-7150

Generations Together was formed in 1978 as a single program, the Senior Citizen School Volunteer Program. Since then, it has grown into a family of programs that foster mutually beneficial contact between the generations. GT is now a direct-service provider and a consulting/training organization as well. It operates programs with community groups and older adults in western Pennsylvania and trains school, church, and community groups in other locales to begin intergenerational programs. Among GT's programs are Youth in Service to Elders, Senior Mentors, Telephone Reassurance for children, and Curriculum on Aging, for teachers of grades one through six. GT rents and sells videos demonstrating several of its intergenerational projects.

PUBLICATIONS: Among GT's publications are *Exchange: A Newsletter Exchanging Information on Intergenerational Programs* and the publications catalog, which lists reprints of articles on intergenerational programs, bibliographies, manuals, and research studies.

Independent Sector (IS)
Brian O'Connell, President
1828 L Street, NW
Washington, DC 20036
(202) 223-8100

IS is a nonprofit coalition of more than 650 corporate, foundation, and voluntary-organization members. Its mission is to create a forum for the promotion of volunteerism. IS's current program areas include increasing volunteer activity and charitable giving, gathering and disseminating research data on volunteerism in the United States, promoting awareness and willingness to volunteer among students, conducting organizational-effectiveness studies for use by nonprofit and philanthropic organizations, and helping to find solutions to the insurance-liability problems affecting grant makers and grant seekers.

PUBLICATIONS: The publication of books, research reports, directories, and single-topic working papers is an important aspect of Independent Sector's service. One of IS's best-known books is *America's Voluntary Spirit: A Book of Readings,* by

Brian O'Connell. It is a collection of speeches, articles, and papers on volunteerism in the United States. See the Books section of Chapter 5 for more detailed information. The monthly newsletter, *Update,* provides members with legislative reports as well as updates on management and fund-raising trends.

National AIDS Network (NAN)
2033 M Street, NW, Suite 800
Washington, DC 20036
(202) 293-2437

NAN is a support network for organizations that provide community-based AIDS education and services. The agency enables service providers to share hands-on experience and receive technical expertise. It acts as a clearinghouse for information. NAN was started in 1985 by five AIDS service agencies. It now has more than 650 members, among them are independent agencies and programs affiliated with health departments, hospitals, drug-rehabilitation centers, and universities. NAN serves members through four programs. (1) Clearinghouse and Resource Development publishes the *NAN Directory of AIDS Education and Service Organizations* and Technical Assistance Packets that address such concerns as media relations, development of volunteer programs, and state Medicaid waivers. (2) Minority Affairs offers materials and information on services targeted to those minority groups heavily victimized by the AIDS epidemic. (3) Field Resources provides NAN members with support and training in program design, implementation, and evaluation. The annual Skills Building Conference is part of Field Resources. It helps community-based service providers acquire the techniques of effective agency management. (4) Communications and Media Relations helps NAN members foster favorable public climates in local communities for the treatment and prevention of AIDS. NAN membership categories include the community-based organization membership, public-health-department membership, and associate membership.

PUBLICATIONS: NAN publishes *Network News,* the monthly newsletter, "NAN Reports," which include conference proceedings and reports, and special releases on volunteer programs and technical information. Address requests for publication information to the Clearinghouse and Resource Development Program.

National Association of Retired Senior Volunteer Program Directors, Inc. (NARSVPD)
Maureen Mulligan, President
c/o St. Joseph's Hospital and Medical Center
703 Main Street
Paterson, NJ 07503
(201) 881-6536

> As a professional society, NARSVPD serves these objectives: (1) it provides visibility and advocacy for the Retired Senior Volunteer Program (RSVP), (2) it provides a network for communication among RSVP directors and projects, and (3) it is a vehicle for the expression of majority opinion on behalf of RSVP and older Americans to the appropriate governmental agencies. The national agenda of NARSVPD includes professional development of RSVP directors through workshops and training programs of technical assistance, resource development through networking with both the private sector and public agencies, advocacy for older Americans, and communication on issues and ideas relevant to RSVP. Membership stands at 650.

> PUBLICATIONS: The membership newsletter and periodic reports from NARSVPD's Washington representative.

National Association of Senior Companion Project Directors (NASCPD)
Berryl Thompson, President
P.O. Box 1510
Opelousas, LA 70570
(318) 948-3682

> Founded in 1978, NASCPD has 250 members. The organization fosters communication between project directors, organizations, and agencies serving the Senior Companion Projects. Among the goals of NASCPD are support and exchange of services among programs benefiting the aging, prevention of duplication of services, expansion of opportunities for senior companions worldwide, and increased stipends for volunteers. Services to members include professional training and development, statistical data for use in program development, and awards for excellence.

> PUBLICATIONS: NASCPD publishes a newsletter for its members.

United Way of America (UWA)
William Aramony, President

701 North Fairfax Street
Alexandria, VA 22314-2045
(703) 836-7100

This is the national service and training center for the 2,300 local United Ways. The UWA provides the following services for its local members: it secures cooperation with other national charities and the labor movement; develops fund-raising techniques; offers administrative and financial services; institutes state and federal government-relations programs; incorporates information-technology advancements; and provides personnel services, training programs, and volunteer-outreach services. Among UWA's direct services are the National Academy for Voluntarism, the Second Century Management System, the Human Care Network Information Services, and Private Sector Initiatives Network. The National Academy for Voluntarism trains professionals from local United Ways and agencies through classes, workshops, and roundtables. The academy provides executive training as well. The Second Century Management System is a resource-development and volunteer-tracking computer software package designed for use with certain types of computer systems. Human Care Network Information Services (HCN) is a nationwide telecommunications network designed for United Ways and other human-service organizations. It is a vehicle for gathering and sharing data. HCN subscribers receive access to a set of office-automation tools; to human-service databases relevant to United Ways; and on-line services, including UWA newsletters, press releases, catalogs, schedules, directories, and bulletin boards. The Private Sector Initiatives Network is a computerized access system to private-sector community-project summaries from across the United States that have demonstrated success. One of the project categories covered by the network is volunteerism. For a complete description of the Private Sector Initiatives Network, please see the Electronic Media section in Chapter 6.

Local United Way organizations serve their communities through networks of volunteers and local charities. They are best known for their united fund-raising campaigns on behalf of local service agencies. Other community United Way activities include assembling task forces to solve problems, assessing community needs, recruiting and training volunteers, and referring individuals to needed services. Local United Ways often help match volunteers with service positions in their communities through newsletters, telephone referral, and computerized matching services.

PUBLICATIONS: UWA publishes a vast number of training and how-to materials for every aspect of human services. The 90-page catalog describes offerings that include audiovisual and computerized materials as well as printed texts. UWA's president, William Aramony, is the author of *The United Way,* an account of the organization's first one hundred years. For a more detailed description of this book, please see the Books section of Chapter 5. The UWA's 1988 publication, *Retirees: A Profile of the 55-and-Over Market,* gives a wealth of statistical and narrative information about this age group. A summary of this publication is in the Booklets, Manuals, and Pamphlets section of Chapter 5.

VOLUNTEER–The National Center
Frank H. Bailey, Executive Director
1111 North Nineteenth Street, Suite 500
Arlington, VA 22209
(703) 276-0542

The goals of VOLUNTEER are to help more people become effectively involved in volunteering, to help develop and sustain local volunteer efforts, to increase public awareness and understanding of the importance of volunteering, and to demonstrate innovative ways of applying volunteer energies to specific problems. VOLUNTEER was incorporated as a private, nonprofit corporation in 1979. It provides technical assistance and training for volunteer centers and for corporations with employee-volunteer programs. VOLUNTEER's services include information on volunteering for nonprofit organizations, business, government, and the media; support for the development of the nearly 400 local Volunteer Centers in the United States; consultation to corporations seeking to encourage volunteerism among their employees; VOLNET, an electronic news service that encourages networking among voluntary organizations (for a description, please refer to the Electronic Media section of Chapter 6); cosponsorship (with ACTION) of the President's Volunteer Action Awards; sponsorship of National Volunteer Week; the annual VOLUNTEER Conference offering training for private- and public-sector volunteer leaders; and the Private Sector Initiatives Database, a vehicle for retrieving information on projects that involve volunteers in solving local problems (for a more detailed description, please refer to the Electronic Media section of Chapter 6). The VOLUNTEER Associate Membership is for individuals, nonprofit organizations, and government agencies. Membership benefits include subscriptions to *Voluntary Action Leadership* and *Volunteering,* both described below; a registration discount on VOLUNTEER's annual conference; billing privileges on catalog orders; access to VOLUNTEER's national volunteerism library; and other information services.

PUBLICATIONS: VOLUNTEER's publications program is extensive. It includes *Volunteering,* the bimonthly newsletter that contains national and local news of interest to the organization's membership, *Voluntary Action Leadership,* a quarterly magazine, which is a professional resource for volunteer-program administrators (for further details on this publication, please see the Periodicals section of Chapter 5), and *Volunteer Readership,* the annual catalog offering volunteer recognition, recruitment, and promotion items as well as books, manuals, and videotapes on all aspects of volunteerism.

State Volunteer-Network Organizations

This state-by-state listing of volunteer-network organizations is a starting point for locating local and regional volunteer opportunities. For more comprehensive information, refer to the *1989 Volunteer Center Associate Member Directory,* as described in the Directories section of Chapter 5; contact VOLUNTEER–The National Center through the listing provided in this chapter; or refer to the telephone directory Yellow Pages under the listings suggested on page 136 in Chapter 2.

Alabama

United Way Volunteer and Information
   Center
Jo H. Greer, Voluntarism Coordinator
3600 Eighth Avenue, South, Suite 504
Birmingham, AL 35222
(205) 251-5131, ext. 53

Volunteer Mobile
Penny Dendy, Director
2504 Dauphin Street, Suite K
Mobile, AL 36606
(205) 479-0631

The Voluntary Action Center
Doci Haslam, Executive Director
2125 East South Boulevard
P.O. Box 11044
Montgomery, AL 36116-0044
(205) 284-0006

Alaska

Volunteer Opportunities/United Way
Sharon Richards, Director
1901 South Bragaw, Suite 102
Anchorage, AK 99504
(907) 272-5579

Arizona

Volunteer Center of Maricopa County
Lucia Causey, Executive Director
1515 East Osborn
Phoenix, AZ 85014
(602) 263-9736

Volunteer Center
Ellen Hargis, Executive Director
3813 East Second Street
Tucson, AZ 85716
(602) 327-6207

Arkansas

Voluntary Action Center
Debra Milam, Director
P.O. Box 3257
Little Rock, AR 72203
(501) 376-4567

California

Volunteer Bureau of Fresno, Inc.
Clifford T. Stevenson, Executive
  Director
2135 Fresno Street, Suite 304
Fresno, CA 93721
(209) 237-3101

Volunteer Center of Los Angeles
Betty Kozasa, Acting Executive Director
621 South Virgil
Los Angeles, CA 90005
(213) 736-1311

Volunteer Center of Sacramento
Mary E. Vogee-Fitzpatrick, Director
331 J Street, Suite 203
Sacramento, CA 95814
(916) 441-4357

Volunteer Center of San Francisco
LeRoy W. Williams, Executive Director
1090 Sansome Street
San Francisco, CA 94111
(415) 982-8999

Volunteer Center Orange
  County–Central/South
Carol R. Stone, Executive Director
1000 East Santa Ana Boulevard,
  Suite 300
Santa Ana, CA 92701
(714) 953-5757

Colorado

Center for Information & Volunteer
  Action
Dorothy Coppock, Executive Director
P.O. Box 1248
Aspen, CO 81612
(303) 925-7887

Volunteer Center–Mile High United
  Way
Susan Boyd, Director
2505 Eighteenth Street
Denver, CO 80211-3907
(303) 433-8383

Connecticut

The Volunteer Bureau of Greater
   Danbury
Bobbi Feinson, Executive Director
337 Main Street
Danbury, CT 06810
(203) 797-1154

Voluntary Action Center for the Capitol
   Region, Inc.
M. Deborah Walsh, Executive Director
880 Asylum Avenue
Hartford, CT 06105
(203) 247-2580

Voluntary Action Center of SE
   Connecticut
Darbee Percival, Executive Director
100 Broadway
Norwich, CT 06360
(203) 887-2519

District of Columbia

Volunteer Clearinghouse of D.C.
James R. Lindsay, Executive Director
1313 New York Avenue, NW, Suite 303
Washington, DC 20005
(202) 638-2664

Florida

The Volunteer Center of Alachua
   County
Darlene S. Kostrub, Executive Director
220 North Main Street
P.O. Box 14561
Gainesville, FL 32602
(904) 378-2552

Volunteer Referral Service/United Way
   of Dade County
Constance V. Krell, Director
600 Brickell Avenue
Miami, FL 33131
(305) 579-2300

Volunteer Center of Central Florida
Pat Schuler, Executive Director
1900 North Mills Avenue, Suite One
Orlando, FL 32803
(407) 896-0945

Volunteer Center of Hillsboro County
Betty Tribble, Executive Director
4023 North Armenia Street, Suite 300
Tampa, FL 33607
(813) 878-2500

Georgia

Voluntary Action Center of United Way
Sue Riley, Director of Community
   Services
500 North Slappey Boulevard
P.O. Box 3609
Albany, GA 31706
(912) 883-6700

Volunteer Resource Center
Linda D. Pulley, Director
P.O. Box 2692
Atlanta, GA 30371
(404) 527-7346

Hawaii

Voluntary Action Center of Oahu
Joan Naguwa, Director
200 North Vineyard Boulevard, Room
   603
Honolulu, HI 96817
(808) 536-7234

Idaho

Lewis-Clark Volunteer Bureau
Melissa Brown, Director
413 Main, Room 210
Lewiston, ID 83501
(208) 746-0136

Illinois

Volunteer Center–United Way/Crusade
  of Mercy
Robert A. Adams, Manager
125 South Clark Street
Chicago, IL 60603-4012
(312) 580-2723

Community Volunteer Center
Lila G. Christensen, Director
Lincoln Land Community College
Shepherd Road
Springfield, IL 62794-9256
(217) 786-2430

Indiana

Volunteer Action Center
Martha R. Bolyard, Director
1828 North Meridian Street
Indianapolis, IN 46202
(317) 923-1466

Community Resource Center of
  St. Joseph County, Inc.
Shelly Lindsay, Executive Director
914 Lincolnway West
South Bend, IN 46601
(219) 232-2522

Iowa

Volunteer Center of United Way of
  Central Iowa
Carol Clift, Director
1111 Ninth Street, Suite 300
Des Moines, IA 50314
(515) 246-6545

The Voluntary Action Center of
  Muscatine
Katrina Wisniewski, Director
501 Sunset Drive
Muscatine, IA 52761
(319) 263-0959

Kansas

Volunteer Center of Topeka, Inc.
Nancy Shaughnessy, Executive Director
4125 Gage Center Drive, Suite 214
Topeka, KS 66604
(913) 272-8890

United Way Volunteer Center
Deedee Evans, Director
212 North Market, Suite 200
Wichita, KS 67202
(316) 267-1321

Kentucky

Volunteer Center of the Bluegrass
Lenora Isenhour, Executive Director
2029 Bellefonte Drive
Lexington, KY 40503
(606) 278-6258

United Way Voluntary Action Center
Elizabeth Marquardt, Director
334 East Broadway
P.O. Box 4488
Louisville, KY 40204-0488
(502) 583-2821

Louisiana

Volunteer Baton Rouge
Noel Parnell, Director
8776 Bluebonnet Boulevard
Baton Rouge, LA 70810
(514) 767-1698

United Way Volunteer Center
Sydney S. Heard, Director
1300 Hudson Lane, Suite 7
Monroe, LA 71201
(318) 325-3869

Volunteer & Information Agency, Inc.
Gail McGlothin, Volunteer Center
  Director
4747 Earhart Boulevard, Suite 111
New Orleans, LA 70125
(504) 488-4636

Maine

The Center for Voluntary Action of
   Greater Portland
Anita J. Murray, Director
233 Oxford Street
Portland, ME 04101
(207) 874-1015

Maryland

Volunteer Center of Frederick County
Jeannine Myers, Executive Director
22 South Market Street
Frederick, MD 21701
(301) 663-0011

Massachusetts

Voluntary Action Center/United Way of
   Massachusetts Bay
Christine G. Franklin, Director
Two Liberty Square
Boston, MA 02109
(617) 482-8370

Michigan

The Center for Volunteer/United
   Community Services of Metro Detroit
Maurice P. Wesson, Manager
1212 Greswold at State
Detroit, MI 48226-1899
(313) 226-9429

Volunteer Center/United Way of Kent
   County
Vicki J. Weaver, Director
500 Commerce Building
Grand Rapids, MI 49503
(616) 459-6281

Minnesota

Voluntary Action Center
Marsha Eisenberg, Director
402 Ordean Building
424 West Superior Street
Duluth, MN 55802
(218) 726-4776

Voluntary Action Center of the St. Paul
   Area
Kathleen Jowett, Executive Director
Bolander Building, Suite 127
251 Starkey Street
St. Paul, MN 55107
(612) 227-3938

Mississippi

Volunteer Center of United Way
Doris Barwick, Director
P.O. Drawer 23169
Jackson, MS 39225-3169
(601) 762-8557

Missouri

Volunteer Center—Heart of America
   United Way
Pat Cundiff, Executive Director
605 West Forty-seventh Street, Suite 300
Kansas City, MO 64112
(816) 531-1945

United Way of Greater St. Louis VAC
Barbara Henning, Vice-President
1111 Olive
St. Louis, MO 63101
(314) 421-0700

Montana

Community Help Line
Shayna R. Dickey, Executive Director
113 Sixth Street, North
Great Falls, MT 59401
(406) 761-6010

Nebraska

United Way Volunteer Bureau
Jamesena Moore, Director
1805 Harney Street
Omaha, NE 68102
(402) 342-8232, ext. 531

Nevada

United Way Volunteer Bureau
Jacqueline Matthews, Director
1055 East Tropicana, Suite 300
Las Vegas, NV 89119
(702) 798-4636

New Hampshire

Voluntary Action Center
Linda Kasiewicz, Program Manager
102 North Main Street
Manchester, NH 03102
(603) 668-8601

New Jersey

The Volunteer Center of Atlantic County
Matt Custer, President
1125 Atlantic Avenue, Fourth Floor
Atlantic City, NJ 08401
(609) 344-7011

Volunteer Center of Greater Essex
    County, Inc.
Joyce Wibbelt, Executive Director
303-309 Washington Street, Fifth Floor
Newark, NJ 07102
(201) 622-3737

New Mexico

The Volunteer Center of Albuquerque
Helen Renwick, Executive Director
302 Eighth Street, NW
P.O. Box 1767
Albuquerque, NM 87103
(505) 247-3671

New York

The Volunteer Center of Albany, Inc.
Executive Director
340 First Street
Albany, NY 12206
(518) 424-2061

Volunteer Center of the United Way of
    Buffalo/Erie Counties
Rita Hardy, Volunteer Center
    Coordinator
742 Delaware Avenue
Buffalo, NY 14209
(716) 887-2692

Mayor's Voluntary Action Center
Winifred L. Brown, Executive Director
61 Chambers Street
New York, NY 10007
(212) 566-5950

Volunteer Center, Inc.
Jean J. Greene, Director
115 East Jefferson Street, Suite 300
Syracuse, NY 13202
(315) 474-7011

North Carolina

United Way/Voluntary Action Center
Lisa Martinez, Director
301 South Brevard Street
Charlotte, NC 28202
(704) 372-7170

United Way of Wake County Voluntary
    Action Center
Stephen Dudek, Director
1100 Wake Forest Road
P.O. Box 11426
Raleigh, NC 27604
(919) 833-5739

North Dakota

United Way's Volunteer Center
Melinda S. Hohncke, Director
315 North Eighth Street
P.O. Box 1609
Fargo, ND 58107-1609
(701) 237-5050

Ohio

The Volunteer Center, United Way
    Services
Kenneth J. Kovach, Director
3100 Euclid Avenue
Cleveland, OH 44115
(216) 361-1010

Voluntary Action Center of United Way
Delores J. Jividan, Director
184 Salem Avenue
Dayton, OH 45406
(513) 225-3066

Voluntary Action Center
Christine Kolasinski, Director
One Stranahan Square, Suite 141
Toledo, OH 43604
(419) 244-3063

Oregon

Volunteer Bureau of Greater Portland
Phyllis Proppe, Executive Director
718 West Burnside, Room 404
Portland, OR 97209
(503) 222-1355

Pennsylvania

Volunteer Action Council, Inc.
Patricia McBee, Executive Director
Seven Benjamin Franklin Parkway
Philadelphia, PA 19103
(215) 568-6360

Volunteer Action Center/United Way of
    Allegheny County
Lavera S. Brown, Program Director
200 Ross Street
P.O. Box 735
Pittsburgh, PA 15230
(412) 261-6010, ext. 242

Voluntary Action Center of
    Northeastern Pennsylvania
Jim Gallagher, Executive Director
225 North Washington Avenue
Scranton, PA 18503
(717) 347-5616

Rhode Island

Volunteers in Action, Inc.
Betsy Aldrich Garland, Executive
    Director
229 Waterman Street
Providence, RI 02906
(401) 421-6547

South Carolina

VAC-Trident United Way
Leslie S. Davis, Director
1069 King Street
P.O. Box 2696
Charleston, SC 29403
(803) 723-1676

United Way Voluntary Action Center
Laura E. Truelove, Director
1800 Main Street
P.O. Box 152
Columbia, SC 29202
(803) 733-5400

United Way of the Piedmont/Volunteer
    Center
Joyce Daniels, Director
101 East St. John Street, Suite 307
P.O. Box 5624
Spartanburg, SC 29304
(803) 582-7556

South Dakota

Volunteer & Information Center
Nancee Riveland, Executive Director
304 South Phillips, Suite 310
Sioux Falls, SD 57102
(605) 339-4357

Tennessee

Volunteer Center of United Way of
    Greater Knoxville, Inc.
Donna Deichert, Director
1514 East Fifth Avenue
P.O. Box 326
Knoxville, TN 37901-0326
(615) 523-9135

Volunteer Center of Memphis
Marion E. Gruber, Executive Director
263 South McLean Boulevard
Memphis, TN 38104
(901) 276-8655

Volunteer Center—United Way of
    Nashville
Anne Layman, Director
250 Venture Circle
P.O. Box 24667
Nashville, TN 37202
(615) 255-8501

Texas

Volunteer Action Center of the United
    Way
Vicki Brooks, Executive Director
2207 Line Avenue
P.O. Box 3069
Amarillo, TX 79116-3069
(806) 376-6714

Volunteer Center of the Coastal Bend
Gilna Nance, Executive Director
1721 South Brownlee Boulevard
Corpus Christi, TX 78404
(512) 887-4545

Volunteer Center of Dallas County
Julie Thomas, Executive Director
2816 Swiss
Dallas, TX 75204
(214) 744-1194

Volunteer Bureau of United Way
Cynthia Gongaware, Director
1918 Texas Street
P.O. Box 3488
El Paso, TX 79923
(915) 532-4919

The Volunteer Center of the Texas Gulf
    Coast
Carrie Moffitt, Executive Director
3100 Timmons Lane, Suite 100
Houston, TX 77027
(713) 965-0031

United Way Volunteer Center
Evelyn Walsworth, Director
P.O. Box 898
San Antonio, TX 78293-0898
(512) 224-5000, ext. 263

Utah

United Way Community Services, Inc.
Lorri A. Hirst, Executive Director
60 East 100 South
P.O. Box 135
Provo, UT 84603
(801) 374-8108

Voluntary Action Center of Community
    Services Council
Rita Inoway, Director
212 West 1300 South
Salt Lake City, UT 84115
(801) 486-2136

Virginia

Volunteer Action Center of South
   Hampton Roads
Lenora D. Mathews, Executive Director
253 West Freemason Street
Norfolk, VA 23510
(804) 624-2403

Volunteer Center of United Way of
   Greater Richmond
Elena Delgado, Director
4001 Fitzhugh Avenue
P.O. Box 6649
Richmond, VA 23230-0049
(804) 353-2000, ext. 224

Voluntary Action Center
Geri E. Muller, VAC Coordinator
920 South Jefferson Street
P.O. Box 496
Roanoke, VA 24003
(703) 985-0131

Washington

United Way Volunteer Center of King
   County
Clydean Zuckerman, Director
107 Cherry Street
Seattle, WA 98104
(206) 461-3751

United Way's Volunteer Center
Jacque Ferrell, Coordinator
P.O. Box 326
Spokane, WA 99210-0326
(509) 838-6581

Wisconsin

Voluntary Action Center/United Way of
   Dane County
Kathy Martinson, Director
2059 Atwood Avenue
Madison, WI 53704
(608) 246-4380

Volunteer Center of Greater Milwaukee,
   Inc.
Virginia Cronk, Executive Director
600 East Mason Street
Milwaukee, WI 53202
(414) 273-7887

Wausau Area Volunteer Exchange
Carole W. Hubbard, Executive Director
407 Grant Street
Wausau, WI 54401
(715) 845-5279

Wyoming

Volunteer Information Center
Robert Banker, Director
406 East Seventeenth Street
P.O. Box 404
Cheyenne, WY 82003
(307) 632-4132

Chapter 5

Reference Material

This chapter describes a collection of resources for volunteers, volunteer leaders, program directors and planners, human-service providers, researchers, and policymakers. Some of the items are practical how-to guides; others are background pieces on volunteerism, aging, and related social issues. Unless the potential audience for a resource is obvious from its title, the annotation will suggest who might find it to be of particular value.

The number of books available on volunteer and agency management is huge. The same is true of magazine articles on volunteers and volunteer programs. It was necessary to be selective in making the choices for this bibliography. The titles here are representative and, in the author's opinion, are of sound quality.

Prices are included whenever possible and reflect the most current information available. Because book prices are subject to change at the publisher's discretion, those listed here serve as a guide for purchasing decisions. If a price is not given, it is likely that the book is out of print. In that case, it is probably available on loan through libraries.

Books

Anthes, Earl, Jerry Cronin, and Michael Jackson, eds. *The Nonprofit Board Book: Strategies for Organizational Success*. Rev. ed. West Memphis and Hampton, Arkansas: Independent Community Consultants, 1985. 240p. $24.50. ISBN 0-916721-04-3.

> The authors are professionals with experience in all aspects of managing nonprofit organizations. In this book their subjects

include meeting effectiveness, staff-volunteer communications, volunteer roles, and public relations. The diagrams, charts, and worksheets are useful for board retreats and orientations as well as management meetings. The information on board development will be of interest to staff and volunteers alike. The chapters have reading lists and are complete in themselves.

Aramony, William. *The United Way: The Next Hundred Years.* New York: Donald I. Fine, 1987. 127p. $13.95. ISBN 1-55611-039-1.

The author looks at the 100-year-old United Way movement in the United States from a unique vantage point. He is its president and a 30-year veteran of the organization. The book is inspiring and well written with dozens of stories verifying the presence and value of the volunteer spirit in local communities. One chapter recounts stories about innovative fund-raising events. While the book's primary intent is to showcase the United Way's history and achievements, it shows the power of volunteerism and describes creative possibilities for fund-raising that any reader will find useful.

Bird, Caroline. *The Good Years: Your Life in the Twenty-First Century.* New York: E. P. Dutton, 1983. 244p. ISBN 0-525-93284-4.

This is a highly readable work for laypersons and professionals by an author who is respected for her ability to document and interpret social change. Bird makes a convincing case for optimism about the aging of U.S. society. In the chapter "Human Work," she cites case after case of older persons who embark on new ventures as volunteers, entrepreneurs, and employees. For the future, she proposes ways to channel life experience into socially productive work such as "systems patching," for example. The book is well documented and contains an index.

Bolles, Richard N. *The Three Boxes of Life and How To Get Out of Them.* Rev. ed. Berkeley: Ten Speed Press, 1981. 466p. $11.95. ISBN 0-913-668-58-3.

In this life-planning guide, Bolles makes a sound case for incorporating a balance of work, learning, and leisure into each stage of life. The chapter on retirement explores methods for designing meaning into life by mixing paid or voluntary work, lifelong learning, and fun. The sections on physical, financial, emotional, and spiritual survival offer self-discovery exercises and ample references to publications, organizations, and programs to use for information gathering and action planning. In a friendly, easy-to-follow manner, the author guides the reader to a full view of the possibilities for purpose and satisfaction in adulthood.

Chambre, Susan M. *Good Deeds in Old Age: Volunteering by the New Leisure Class*. Lexington, MA: D. C. Heath, 1987. 135p. $25. ISBN 0-669-13091-5.

> This study is based on a 1982 survey of older adults conducted by Louis Harris and Associates for the National Council on the Aging. The findings conclude that individuals with strong work and family ties are more likely to volunteer and that volunteering is more a result of high life satisfaction than a contributor to it. Based on her findings, Chambre makes practical recommendations on recruiting older volunteers and designing volunteer jobs. The book will be a helpful resource to program planners and policymakers. Extensive bibliographies and an index are included.

Committee on an Aging Society. *Productive Roles in an Older Society*. Washington, DC: National Academy Press, 1986. 154p. ISBN 0-309-03637-2.

> One chapter in this collection of essays addresses volunteerism as a productive role for elder Americans. The author, Jarold Kieffer, suggests that older Americans are a potential resource for easing the burden of reduced public funding for community social services. He addresses the barriers to such volunteer participation—staff resistance, inadequate transportation and training—and proposes solutions. Kieffer spells out specific areas of need for volunteers, one of which is supportive services to the over-age-85 population. The book has an index and extensive demographic data. Each chapter has a bibliography.

Driver, David E. *The Good Heart: A Guide to Volunteering*. Chicago: Noble Press, 1989. 286p. $18.95 (paperback $11.95). ISBN 0-9622683-0-5.

> This is a step-by-step plan for identifying expectations for, and finding, the right volunteer job. Nine major social problems that rely on volunteer service are outlined, including homelessness,

family violence, and the abandoned elderly. It contains profiles of volunteers, programs, and volunteer jobs. The book concludes with a directory of agencies, a list of references, and an index. The author came out of poverty, with the help of volunteers, to achieve a successful career as a stockbroker. His story therefore makes a strong case for the power of volunteers to help others change their lives.

Duca, Diane J. *Nonprofit Boards: A Practical Guide to Roles, Responsibilities, and Performance.* Phoenix: Oryx Press, 1986. 228p. $28.50. ISBN 0-89774-231-1.

> Starting with the board's legal and moral obligations, Duca explains the steps in developing a well-functioning board of directors. For existing boards, she offers guidelines for productive meetings and leadership techniques that sustain volunteer commitment. Ample subheadings; illustrations; checklists; case studies; and sample minutes, board job descriptions, agendas, and budgets make this a useful volume. The annotated bibliography includes such categories as leadership, fund-raising, and group dynamics.

Dychtwald, Ken, and Joe Flower. *Age Wave: The Challenges and Opportunities of an Aging America.* Los Angeles: Jeremy P. Tarcher, 1989. 380p. $19.95. ISBN 0-87477-441-1.

> The authors demonstrate how the "age wave" holds the promise of a more humane society. As a noted gerontologist and consultant in aging issues, Dychtwald brings a wealth of experience and knowledge to the book. In the section on volunteering, the authors assert that a significant number of older Americans are more interested in giving than in taking. They verify this with examples of the diverse volunteer activity among older adults. A particularly unique aspect of this section is the set of proposals for community volunteer programs of the future. *Age Wave* is highly readable and informative for lay and professional audiences. It has chapter-by-chapter notes and an index.

Flanagan, Joan. *The Successful Volunteer Organization: Getting Started and Getting Results in Nonprofit, Charitable, Grass Roots, and Community Groups.* Arlington, VA: VOLUNTEER—The National Center, 1981. 376p. $9.50. ISBN 0-318-17155-4.

"How do you build an organization worth raising money for?" is the theme of the book. In "Getting Started," Flanagan explains how to make a good idea into an organization. "Getting Results" addresses committee formation, fund-raising, and hiring staff. "Getting Organized" covers job descriptions and preparing board reports. "Getting Advice" extensively lists free literature and services. Each chapter closes with how-to steps for achieving the task it describes, for example, "Steps to Hiring and Supervising Staff." An annotated bibliography is keyed to each chapter. The book is an excellent resource for professional staff and volunteers.

Henson, Sarah, and Bruce Larson. *Risk Management: Strategies for Managing Volunteer Programs.* Walla Walla, WA: Macduff/Bunt Publishing (821 Lincoln, Walla Walla, WA 99362), 1988. 132p. $19.95 ($24.25 if ordered by mail). ISBN 0-945795-04-1.

This how-to book is coauthored by a volunteer-program manager and an attorney. The layperson can readily grasp their clear explanations of tort claims; liability management; risk-reduction strategies; the importance of bylaws, policies, and procedures; and how to create a "paper-trail" or essential documentation of management decisions. Each chapter has worksheets for risk-management teams and sample documents from well-managed programs. Many checklists, a chapter-by-chapter bibliography, and a glossary make this manual a valuable reference for program staff and volunteers alike.

Kouri, Mary K. *Elderlife: A Time To Give—A Time To Receive.* Denver, CO: Human Growth & Development Associates, 1985. 79p. $10. ISBN 0-9616626-0-3.

Using 12 "Life Design Tools" the author guides readers through a series of practical steps for making transitions from one chapter of life to the next. The workbook is particularly suited for persons who are looking ahead to retirement and for those who are seeking new directions in their seventh and eighth decades of life. Readers will find the tools helpful whether they aspire to community service, employment, or realizing long-held dreams for self-development. Volunteer leaders can use the Life Design Tools in matching volunteers with jobs and in planning training programs to fit their volunteers' learning styles. Profiles of older adults and a reading list are included.

Macduff, Nancy. *Building Effective Volunteer Committees*. Walla Walla, WA: Macduff/Bunt Associates (821 Lincoln, Walla Walla, WA 99362), 1986. 82p. $11.95 ($16.25 if ordered by mail). ISBN 0-945795-01-7.

> This book outlines ten steps for building effective committees, the backbone of volunteer work. In detail, the chapters explain how to recruit the right people, write guidelines, establish annual work plans, hold members accountable for their responsibilities, and evaluate individuals and committee work. Each chapter has forms suitable for copying and actually using in committee meetings. The material is clearly presented. Humor and practical examples make this book easy to read and its sound guidance easy to remember.

————. *Volunteer Recruiting & Retention: A Marketing Approach*. Walla Walla, WA: Macduff/Bunt Associates (821 Lincoln, Walla Walla, WA 99362), 1985. 196p. $24.95 ($30.25 if ordered by mail). ISBN 0-945795-00-9.

> Macduff explains the book's objective in her introduction: "The marketing strategy of profit making business is wedded to the theories and practicality of adult development and learning. It is an attempt to join the best of both worlds for the effective delivery of program services through the efforts of volunteers." The section on recruitment covers needs assessments and using volunteer-recruitment teams. The elements of volunteer retention include interviewing, volunteer evaluation, and training. Worksheets, sample forms, and bibliographies make this publication a practical workbook for agency staff and volunteer leaders.

Moody, Harry R. *Abundance of Life: Human Development Policies for an Aging Society*. New York: Columbia University Press, 1988. 307p. $37.50. ISBN 0-231-06592-2.

> Ethicist Harry Moody challenges the view that older adults are to be counted as nonproductive and dependent. He argues for a broad vision of productivity that values "nonmonetized" contributions such as volunteerism, mutual self-help, and creative projects. The chapters "Late Life and Uses of Time," "Mediating Structures," and "Mutual Self-Help" are of special interest to policymakers, human-service professionals, and older adults who seek a new vision of the productive possibilities for today's longer life expectancy. Each chapter has extensive notes and bibliographic references. The book has an index.

Moore, Larry F., ed. *Motivating Volunteers: How the Rewards of Unpaid Work Can Meet People's Needs*. Vancouver, British Columbia: Vancouver Volunteer Centre, 1985. 264p. ISBN 0-920447-00-7.

> In Part One volunteer-action practitioners and scholars explain the theories of volunteer motivation. Practical applications are presented in the form of guidelines for volunteer-job design and training. Steps for analyzing and meeting volunteer needs are explained. In Part Two selected papers explore various aspects of volunteer motivation. One research finding indicates that, although self-interest is present, concern for others remains a constant in volunteer motivation. Each chapter has a list of references.

Morrison, Emily Kittle. *Working with Volunteers: Skills for Leadership*. Tucson: Fisher Books, 1988. 251p. $9.95. ISBN 1-55561-015-3.

> The author calls on her background in adult education and volunteer leadership for the techniques she presents in this book. She starts with a brief overview of volunteerism. From there she offers practical how-tos on running meetings, managing group process, motivation, communication, problem solving, management by objectives, publicity, and career development through volunteerism. Program directors and volunteer leaders will find this a useful publication. The book has an index. The bibliography is arranged by subject headings: leadership, group process, board meetings, communication, and time management.

O'Connell, Brian, ed. *America's Voluntary Spirit: A Book of Readings*. New York: The Foundation Center, 1983. 461p. $19.95. ISBN 0-87954079-6. Paperback $14.95. ISBN 0-87954-081-8.

> This is a collection of 45 essays on volunteerism in the United States compiled by one of the recognized leaders in the field. O'Connell's criteria for selecting pieces to include were "quality; representativeness, including different perspectives; [and] long-term relevance, not dated or time limited." Among the authors and sources are *McGuffey's Reader,* Ralph Waldo Emerson, Mary McLeod Bethune, Erma Bombeck, and John Gardner. As an overview of the voluntary movement in the United States and the diverse viewpoints on the topic, this is an excellent resource. An index and 590-item bibliography are included.

O'Connell, Brian, and Ann Brown O'Connell. *Volunteers in Action.* New York: The Foundation Center, 1989. 346p. $24.95. ISBN 0-87954-291-8. Paperback $19.95. ISBN 0-87954-292-6.

> This book gives a close-up view of volunteerism in personal and community lives. Part One is a brief essay on the spirit and power of volunteerism in U.S. society. The seven chapters in Part Two tell the stories of hundreds of people who serve others in schools, cemeteries, hospitals, community centers, on mountain tops, and every other conceivable location. Part Three, "Becoming Part of the Action," offers suggestions on becoming a volunteer. Part Four describes programs that initiate youngsters into the spirit of volunteerism; intergenerational projects are among the examples. A comprehensive index includes subjects, proper names, and programs.

Pell, Arthur R. *Recruiting, Training and Motivating Volunteers.* Babylon, NY: Pilot Books (103 Cooper Street, Babylon, NY 11702), 1989. 61p. $4.95. ISBN 0-87576-141-0.

> This basic guide to working with volunteers is written in short sections. Each one is well marked for quick reference by the reader who might wish to gather tips on just one aspect of working with volunteers. The information is practical, frequently offered in the form of "dos" and "don'ts." The topics are recruiting volunteers, interviewing and selecting volunteers, orientation and training, supervision and leadership, handling problems, getting ideas across, and motivating volunteers.

Pifer, Alan, and Lydia Bronte, eds. *Our Aging Society: Paradox and Promise.* New York: W. W. Norton, 1986. 438p. $22.45. ISBN 0-393-02299-4. Paperback $12.70. ISBN 0-393-30334-9.

> The authors of these 19 essays are experts from various disciplines, including economics, health care, social policy, ethics, sociology, education, and human development. Jacob Siegal and Cynthia Taeuber's contribution on demographics is a valuable background piece. The reader who is interested in the potential of volunteerism in the changing society will find the contributions of Alan Pifer, Harry Moody, and Malcolm Morrison of special interest. Each essay has footnotes; the book has an index.

Rydberg, Wayne D., and Linda J. Peterson, eds. *A Look at the Eighties: Crucial Environmental Factors Affecting Volunteerism*. Appleton, WI: Aid Association for Lutherans, 1980. 79p.

> The Aid Association for Lutherans commissioned four experts from agency and academic backgrounds to research factors that would affect the future of volunteerism. Gordon Manser, Harleigh Trecker, Ivan Scheier, and Jon Van Til address the impact of inflation, government's changing roles, demographic trends, and volunteer expectations. Manser cites the widespread desire of older Americans to be volunteers as shown in a 1974 Harris survey. Extensive footnotes offer access to other books and papers on volunteerism.

Saccomandi, Pat. *The Volunteer Skillsbank: An Innovative Way To Connect Individual Talents to Community Needs*. Arlington, VA: VOLUNTEER–The National Center, 1980. 154p.

> This how-to manual resulted from the work of a task force of nonprofit agencies concerned about methods of identifying and involving individuals in short-term volunteer assignments. After a thorough explanation of the "skillsbank" concept, the author reviews three skillsbank models. She then explains how to recruit registrants, categorize the skills data, connect registrants with requests for their skills, and manage the system. The appendixes and numerous examples from agency experiences make this an important resource, one of the few in-depth publications on skillsbanks. See Resource Match Software and User's Guide in Chapter 6 for developing a computer-aided skillsbank.

Waldo, Charles N. *A Working Guide for Directors of Not-for-Profit Organizations*. New York: Quorum Books, 1986. 160p. $35. ISBN 089930-091-X.

> This guide is equally useful to prospective and seasoned volunteer and agency directors. The author is a 25-year veteran of volunteer service and consultancy in for-profit and nonprofit organizations. He clearly distinguishes for the reader the differences between board member and staff responsibilities. Waldo describes the range of board duties, which include committee service, ambassadorship for the organization, policy and budget review, long-range planning, and hiring and firing a chief executive officer. The book has a bibliography; each chapter has notes.

Wilson, Marlene. *The Effective Management of Volunteer Programs.*
1976. Reprint. Arlington, VA: VOLUNTEER–The National Center,
9th printing, 1988. 197p. $7.35. ISBN 0-318-17163-5.

> This book's flavor is captured in an excerpt from the foreword:
> "A rare combination of humane and very efficient management
> perspectives." Wilson addresses the following issues: volunteer
> motivation and successful matching of volunteers and jobs; pro-
> gram planning based on needs assessment; volunteer-job design
> and recruitment; techniques and procedures for volunteer inter-
> views and placement; designing creative training experiences for
> volunteer directors, volunteers, and staffs; practical application
> of communication theory; and maintaining vitality in the volun-
> tary organization. Chapters include references, appendixes with
> sample forms, charts, checklists, and worksheets.

———. *Survival Skills for Managers.* 1981. Reprint. Arlington, VA:
VOLUNTEER–The National Center, 4th printing, 1988. 264p. $10.50.
ISBN 0-318-17170-8.

> Wilson, an internationally renowned volunteer and staff trainer,
> dedicates this book to the well-being and effective functioning of
> volunteer-program managers. In readable style, she explores cre-
> ativity, problem solving, power and negotiations, stress and
> conflict management, and time structuring. Charts, diagrams,
> insight exercises, case studies, and reprinted papers make this a
> workbook for both individuals and professional groups. Quotes
> and humorous anecdotes add to the book's appeal. Each chapter
> has references and most have appendixes.

Bibliographies

Derrickson, Margaret Chandler. *The Literature of the Nonprofit Sector:
A Bibliography with Abstracts.* Vol. 1. New York: The Foundation
Center, 1989. 403p. $50. ISBN 0-87954-287-X.

> This comprehensive resource contains 5,000 citations, about
> one-third of which include abstracts. The format amply fulfills
> the author's promise to "provide the user with as many access
> points to the literature as possible." Part One is a bibliography of

literature on philanthropy and foundations. Part Two covers the nonprofit sector. Topics include administration, fund-raising, tax and legal matters, voluntarism, and government funding. Part Three cites reference materials, project reports, and research findings related to philanthropy. Part Four contains subject, author, and title indexes. Part Five describes the Foundation Center's services and lists U.S. libraries holding substantial collections on volunteerism.

Layton, Daphne Niobe. *Philanthropy and Voluntarism: An Annotated Bibliography.* New York: The Foundation Center, 1987. 308p. $18.50. ISBN 0-87954-198-9.

This extensive bibliography is primarily intended for scholars and students of philanthropy. The cited books and articles cover the concept and historical settings and precedents of philanthropy; the relationship of private philanthropy to the state; major manifestations of philanthropic activity; philanthropy in other countries and cultures; key periodicals; and commissions, conferences, and organizational resources in the field. There are 1,614 references; 250 of them are extensively annotated. The book is well written, and the author and subject indexes make the contents highly accessible.

Directories

Many of the directories in this section are available from organizations described in Chapter 4. Those that are not have the ordering information included here.

1989–90 Volunteer Center Associate Member Directory. Arlington, VA: VOLUNTEER–The National Center, 1989. 22p. $5.

This listing of volunteer centers is a resource for individuals and organizations who are seeking program information or networking opportunities. All of the centers listed are associate members of VOLUNTEER–The National Center. Entries are arranged alphabetically by state, with Canadian centers listed at the end. The names of directors are included. The directory is updated periodically. Order number 241.

Anderson, Jay. *The Living History Sourcebook*. Nashville: The
American Association for State and Local History (AASLH), 1985.
469p. $23.95. ISBN 0-910050-75-9.

> Anderson is a scholar of folklore and folk life. He offers a highly
> readable wealth of information on the living-history movement
> ("simulation of life in another time") in the United States.
> Dozens of short descriptions and photos introduce the would-be
> volunteer to living history and furnish valuable data to those
> already involved. The book has sections on museums, events,
> books, articles, magazines, organizations, suppliers, sketch-
> books, films, and simulation games. It is well organized and has
> a glossary and index.

Beckmann, David M., Timothy J. Mitchell, and Linda L. Powers. *The
Overseas List: Opportunities for Living and Working in Developing
Countries*. Rev. ed. Minneapolis: Augsburg, 1985. 224p. $12.95.
ISBN 0-8066-2181-8.

> This is a "comprehensive review of nearly all the ways that U.S.
> citizens come to live or travel in developing countries," with
> emphasis on Christian service. The book lists dozens of volunteer
> and employment opportunities. It offers how-to information on
> locating a suitable placement. While their obvious enthusiasm
> for overseas work is contagious, the authors caution readers
> about its rigors. "First timers" receive tips on locating their first
> assignment abroad and a realistic explanation about the hesi-
> tancy of many organizations to send the inexperienced to other
> countries. Three indexes include "Activities," "Nations and Ter-
> ritories," and "Organizations."

Cohen, Marjorie. *Volunteer! The Comprehensive Guide to Voluntary
Service in the U.S. and Abroad, 1988–1989*. New York: Council on
International Educational Exchange, Commission on Voluntary Service
and Action (Volunteer! Distribution, Box 347, Newton, KS 67114),
1988. 155p. $4.95 plus $1 postage.

> *Volunteer!* is the only comprehensive listing of organizations
> placing and using full-time volunteers. Short- and long-term
> opportunities requiring general to specialized skills are listed.
> The guide includes domestic and overseas projects for persons of
> all ages. Financial requirements and volunteer accommodations

are described. The introductions to voluntary service and application procedures are useful. The index includes organizations and publications, skills, location, length of service, opportunities for volunteers under 18, and opportunities for disabled volunteers. Make checks payable to C.V.S.A.

Directory of Private Services 1988. Nashville, TN: Task Force on Families in Crisis, 1988. 172p. Free.

This is a national directory of family services that are funded by private rather than governmental sources. It clearly specifies which family members it serves—abused children, abused women, or abusers. Individuals and groups interested in volunteer opportunities in this field will find the directory a helpful source of contacts. The listings are arranged alphabetically by state and city. The well-organized format affords the reader ready access to the information about actual and potential volunteer-service opportunities. There is a 1989 appendix to the directory.

Generations Together Publications Catalog. Pittsburgh: Generations Together Publications, 1990. 21p. Free.

The publications listed in this annotated catalog are for persons interested in intergenerational volunteer work in schools and community agencies, child-development and aging programs, the arts, and other fields. The sections list professional papers, journal articles, how-to manuals on program development, curricula for preschool to grade six, teaching and demonstration videos, and annotated bibliographies of children's books with an intergenerational focus.

Growing Together: An Intergenerational Sourcebook. Washington, DC: American Association of Retired Persons, 1985. 96p. Free.

This excellent resource provides a broad view of the scope of intergenerational programs and insight into their benefits for both young and old. Chapters include brief descriptions of successful programs in child care, schools, and community settings. The directory lists organizations, publications, and audiovisuals. It includes an index. Order number PF 3611(586).

Helping Out in the Outdoors: A Directory of Volunteer Work and Internships on America's Public Lands. Washington, DC: American

Hiking Society, 1989. 86p. $3, single issue; $12, two-year subscription.
ISSN 8756-310X.

> This is an annotated listing of more than 1,500 volunteer jobs
> available through the American Hiking Society, Appalachian
> Mountain Club, Student Conservation Association, Sierra Club,
> U.S. Geological Survey, U.S. Fish and Wildlife Service, U.S.
> Bureau of Land Management, and various local groups. The
> information is categorized geographically by region and state.
> Typical jobs are campground hosts, tour guides, trail building
> and maintenance, and conducting environmental-education pro-
> grams. Volunteer accommodations are described for each posi-
> tion. The directory is published semiannually, February and
> September.

Kipps, Harriet Clyde, ed. *Volunteerism: The Directory of
Organizations, Training, Programs and Publications, 1990–91*. 3d ed.
New York: R. R. Bowker, 1990. $95. ISBN 0-8352-2739-1.

> This volume lists more than 5,500 organizations. It lists volun-
> teer resources, programs, and training events. Categories, such
> as drug and alcohol abuse, the family, the handicapped, and
> senior citizens, enable the user to quickly locate topics of interest.
> One chapter covers the various state Governor's Offices on Vol-
> unteerism. This directory can serve as a networking and planning
> tool for organizations.

Laubach Literacy Action Directory. Syracuse, NY: Laubach Literacy
Action, 1989. 91p. $3.65 plus $2 postage.

> This annual publication is a valuable resource to anyone who
> seeks an overview of the literacy movement in the United States.
> State-by-state listings include state organizations, local groups,
> and Laubach-certified literacy trainers. It is an excellent network-
> ing tool for the current and potential volunteer. The directory also
> contains an overview of the Laubach program activities.

Lestz, Gerry. *Farm Museum Directory: A Guide through America's
Farm Past*. 2d ed. Lancaster, PA: Stemgas Publishing (P.O. Box 328,
Lancaster, PA 17603), 1988. 48p. $3.50.

> This directory lists museums in the United States, Canada, and
> England. Each entry has a brief description of that museum's

exhibits and activities. Selected libraries and organizations dedicated to historic preservation are listed as well. Individuals who are interested in volunteering in these settings will find this booklet a valuable tool for making contacts.

McMillon, Bill. *Volunteer Vacations: A Directory of Short-Term Adventures that Will Benefit You . . . and Others,* 2d ed. Chicago: Chicago Review Press, 1989. 280p. $11.95. ISBN 155652-051-4.

> The guide contains an alphabetical listing of service projects in the United States and abroad. Listings offer application instructions, job descriptions, costs to the volunteer, and accommodations. (Changes and additions are noted in the periodic publication, *Volunteer Vacations Update,* referenced in the Newsletters section of this chapter.) Projects include archaeology, scientific research, and work camps. Vignettes written by volunteers give insight into the nature and impact of service experiences. Indexes categorize service projects by location, type of work, cost to the volunteer, season(s) available, and length of service.

National Public Radio Member Stations. Washington, DC: National Public Radio, 1988. Free.

> This pamphlet will be useful to individuals who wish to locate volunteer opportunities with local public radio stations. It lists stations in each city by call letter and number. The listings are updated periodically.

National Voluntary Organizations Active in Disaster. Washington, DC: American Red Cross, 1988. 26p. Free.

> This is a quick-reference guide to voluntary organizations that provide services for disaster victims and/or are active in disaster preparedness and planning. Each listing contains contact information and a description of services offered. Individuals who are considering volunteer service in this field will find this a helpful resource. The American Red Cross prints and updates the booklet periodically.

Volunteers Who Produce Books: Braille, Tape, Large Print. Washington, DC: Library of Congress (National Library Service for the Blind and Physically Handicapped, Library of Congress, Washington, DC 20542), 1988. 95p. Free. ISSN 0193-113X.

This directory, available in large-print and braille formats, lists volunteer groups and individuals who transcribe and record books as well as other reading materials for blind and physically handicapped persons. Listings are alphabetical by state. They include such services as braille transcription, computer-assisted transcription, large-print typing, tape recording, duplication, and binding. The entries also include specialties, music, mathematics, and languages, for example. The directory has separate sections on state special-education contacts and proofreaders certified by the Library of Congress. Periodic updates of the booklet incorporate data submitted by individuals and organizations.

Working Group on Special Collections in Volunteerism. *Volunteerism: A Directory of Special Collections 1988*. Blacksburg, VA: Center for Volunteer Development (Jane P. Janey, Assistant Director for Public Information, Center for Volunteer Development, Continuing Education Center, CVD Suite, Virginia Polytechnic Institute and SU, Blacksburg, VA 24061), 1988. 123p. Free. ISBN 0-940576-07-4.

This directory includes detailed entries describing 102 collections of materials and/or books on volunteerism. Listings cover organizations in the United States and Canada. All the collections are accessible in some way to the public. Information about each collection is classified according to types of materials, key subjects covered, methods of classification, forms of catalogs maintained, types of computer hardware/software used, holdings lists, and services available. The directory contains an index and appendix with additional sources of information.

Periodicals

The Gerontologist
Bimonthly. $45, individual; $75, institution.
The Gerontological Society of America
1275 K Street, NW, Suite 350
Washington, DC 20005-4006

This professional journal contains research studies, book reviews, and audiovisual reviews. The articles are categorized by areas of interest, for example, "care settings and transitions," "social networks," and "practice concepts." Each article has an abstract and a list of key words for convenience in scanning and searching. It is a resource for the person who wishes to keep abreast of trends in the study of aging. Much of the information is directly or indirectly applicable to volunteer-program planning and training.

International Journal of Aging and Human Development
Eight issues per year. $45.60, individual; $96, institution.
Baywood Publishing Company
26 Austin Avenue
P.O. Box 337
Amityville, NY 11701

This journal contains articles and research reports on the psychological and social aspects of aging. Typical subjects are self-esteem; factors that contribute to life satisfaction; and the impact of economics, relationships, life events, social programs, and personality factors on the well-being of older adults. The journal will be helpful to professional staff and researchers.

The Journal of Volunteer Administration
Quarterly. No cost to AVA members; $24 nonmembers.
Association for Volunteer Administration (AVA)
P.O. Box 4584
Boulder, CO 80306

The articles focus on volunteerism in any setting. The subject matter ranges from funding, program management, and trends in volunteerism to program and training models. All types of volunteer activity are covered, including formal and informal, nonprofit, government-related, and business-oriented volunteer activities. Each issue contains book reviews. This is an excellent resource for volunteer leaders and professional staff.

Mature Outlook
Bimonthly. $6, members; $9, nonmembers.
Mature Outlook, Inc.
One North Arlington
1500 West Shure Drive
Arlington Heights, IL 60004

The articles in this magazine focus on healthy life-styles. Issues include interviews with well-known individuals, fitness, volunteer-service opportunities, employment, nutritious cooking and eating, physical appearance, money management, and gardening. The attractive format and generous use of color photos make the magazine visually appealing. The articles are well researched and well written.

Modern Maturity
Bimonthly. $5 AARP membership includes subscription.
American Association of Retired Persons (AARP)
3200 East Carson Street
Lakewood, CA 90712

This magazine carries articles on social, political, and economic trends that affect or interest older adults. Minicourses and book reviews are regular departments. Features on service and volunteerism are frequently published in keeping with AARP's motto: To Serve, Not To Be Served. Each issue has updates on activities of local AARP chapters. *Modern Maturity* is noted for its excellence in editorial content and its accessible format. It is an excellent resource for the professional staff person and lay public as well.

New Choices for the Best Years
Monthly. $15.
P.O. Box 1945
Marion, OH 43305-1945

Each issue features articles on life transitions and trends that affect the lives of older adults and their families. Regular departments include health, money, travel, housing trends, food, and mental well-being. Volunteerism is frequently addressed as an option for productive living. There are regular profiles of volunteers and information on service programs. *New Choices* replaced the periodical *50 Plus* in January 1989.

Voluntary Action Leadership
Quarterly. $20.
VOLUNTEER–The National Center
1111 North Nineteenth Street, Suite 500
Arlington, VA 22209
(703) 276-0542

This journal is for the volunteer-program director or coordinator. The articles address effective management, program planning, volunteer training, and program administration. Professional-development information is included such as job-hunting tips and skill building. Research reports, national news, events calendar, resource information, and opinions are regular departments in each issue.

Volunteer Leader
Quarterly. $8.
American Hospital Association
American Hospital Publishing, Inc.
Circulation Division
211 East Chicago Avenue
Chicago, IL 60611
(312) 440-6800 in Illinois
(800) 621-6902

This newsletter is written for directors of hospital volunteer-service departments and auxiliary officers. It serves as a practical resource for successful management of in-service and community-outreach volunteer programs. Features include information on both long-range planning and day-to-day operations. Articles highlight innovative and outstanding programs and note trends in hospital volunteerism.

Newsletters

Older Americans Report
Business Publishers, Inc.
951 Pershing Drive
Silver Spring, MD 20910-4464
(301) 587-6300

This ten-page weekly publication for aging-services professionals carries news briefs relative to older Americans. For example, it covers legislative and financial developments in the federal volunteer programs that operate under ACTION, the U.S. volunteer agency. In addition to federal and state legislative action, the newsletter's regular categories include "Slants and Trends," "Publications and Resources," and "State and Local News." The cost for a one-year subscription is $251.50, which covers first-class postage. Because of the expense of the publication, *Older Americans Report* is most appropriate for large organizations.

Volunteer Vacations Update
Update Publications
2120 Green Hill Road
Sebastopol, CA 95472
(707) 823-2867

> *Update* is a subscription service that provides the following: up-to-date information on organizations included in *Volunteer Vacations* (referenced in the Directories section of this chapter), information about new organizations not included in *Volunteer Vacations,* press releases from organizations who need volunteers, and ten searches of the *Volunteer Vacations* database during the two-year subscription period. The searches help subscribers connect with volunteer opportunities. Organizational subscribers get 30 database searches per subscription. Individual two-year subscriptions cost $49.95; organizational subscriptions, $89.95. Make checks payable to Update.

Booklets, Manuals, and Pamphlets

AARP Publications & A/V Programs: The Complete Collection.
Washington, DC: American Association of Retired Persons, 1988.
52p. Free.

> This catalog lists more than 250 AARP publications and more than 40 audiovisual programs. The section on volunteerism offers booklets describing AARP's numerous opportunities for volunteer service in local communities. Many of the pieces are for volunteer coordinators. All the publications listed in the catalog are free of charge in limited quantities. Audiovisuals include videotape as well as slide presentations. Allow six to eight weeks for delivery of all orders from AARP. Order number PS0362 (1288) C48.

American Association for International Aging. *The Foster Grandparent Program: A Manual for Planning, Implementing and Operating the Foster Grandparent Program.* Washington, DC: American Association for International Aging, 1988. 53p. $5, plus $1.25 postage.

———. *The Retired Senior Volunteer Program: A Manual for Planning, Implementing and Operating RSVP.* Washington, DC: American Association for International Aging, 1987. 55p. $5, plus $1.25 postage.

———. *The Senior Companion Program: A Manual for Planning, Implementing and Operating the Senior Companion Program.* Washington, DC: American Association for International Aging, 1988. 31p. $5, plus $1.25 postage.

> This series explains how to set up Foster Grandparent Programs, Retired Senior Volunteer Programs, and Senior Companion Programs. While the primary audience for the publications is volunteer directors in other countries, the manuals have received positive response in the United States. Each one is organized as follows: Part One, descriptions of actual projects. Part Two, methods used to develop successful projects in the United States. The quotes and vignettes make lively reading. Sample forms, memos, checklists, and letters offer practical guidance to individuals and organizations who are starting projects. The National Association of Retired Senior Volunteer Program Directors and the National Association of Senior Companion Project Directors collaborated in their production. The manuals may be ordered from 1511 K Street, NW, Suite 443, Washington, DC 20005; (202) 638-6815. The set of three costs $15, which includes postage.

Attitudes of Americans over 45 Years of Age on Volunteerism. Washington, DC: American Association of Retired Persons, 1988. 34p. Free.

> This booklet summarizes the findings of a 1988 survey done for AARP by Hamilton, Frederick, and Schneiders. The results are divided according to age groups, educational levels, and employment status. The findings indicate that 41 percent of adults age 65 and over engage in volunteer work. Their reason for volunteering, as most often cited, is personal enjoyment. Trends point toward increased volunteerism among older adults in the future. The booklet is valuable for its quick access to data on the volunteer activities and attitudes of older Americans. Order by title.

Charitable Contributions. Internal Revenue Service. Free. Forms Distribution Center: for Western U.S., Rancho Cordova, CA 95743-0001; for Central U.S., P.O. Box 9903, Bloomington, IL 61799;

for Eastern U.S., P.O. Box 25866, Richmond, VA 23289;
(800) 424-FORM (3676).

> This seven-page pamphlet is a guide to income-tax deductions
> for contributions and gifts to qualified (nonprofit) organiza-
> tions. It discusses the definitions of, and lists further information
> sources on, qualified organizations. Other topics are: deductible
> and nondeductible contributions, limits on deductibility, figuring
> deductions, record keeping, and reporting deductions. The pub-
> lication will be useful to volunteers and program directors. It is
> updated annually. Order number 526.

*Continuing Choices: A Comprehensive Handbook of Programs for
Work with Older Adults.* New York: National Council of Jewish
Women, 1975. 49p. $5.

> This handbook contains 48 ideas for volunteer projects to bene-
> fit older adults. Examples include employment services, oral-
> history projects, respite care, and building a new cultural image
> of aging and older persons. Each summary contains the objec-
> tive, the project description, the population to be served, exper-
> tise and time commitment required by volunteers, and funding
> requirements. This is a valuable guide for individuals and organi-
> zations because it has a broad range of ideas for simple to com-
> plex services. "While many of the programs ... are geared
> toward assisting the elderly, many of them contain the seeds of
> an opposite and equally important approach—matching the
> skills and experience of the aging with the needs of society at all
> levels," Arthur Fleming said in the foreword.

Giving and Volunteering in the United States: 1988 Edition.
Washington, DC: Independent Sector, 1988. 74p. $25. ISSN:
1040-4082.

> This is a summary of Independent Sector's definitive study of
> volunteer-service activity and monetary giving in the United
> States. The survey was conducted by the Gallup Organization as
> a follow-up to earlier ones in 1985 and 1981. Data was collected
> in 1988 from a representative sample of U.S. citizens age 18 and
> older. The results describe volunteers and their motivations, who
> gives, the amount of time and money different population groups
> give, and the public attitudes toward service activities. More

than 70 tables and ample narrative interpretation make this a highly useful publication. Program planners, policymakers, and program managers will find it important. Order directly from Independent Sector.

How To Publish a Directory of Services for Older Adults. New York: National Council of Jewish Women, 1978. 8p. $5.

The procedures explained in this manual will be useful to any organization or individual who aspires to publish a service directory, even though the primary audience is within the NCJW. The sections include steps for establishing a need, setting up a project committee, creating a budget, getting funding and cosponsors, training volunteers, gathering information, production, and publicity and distribution. Fifteen appendixes contain worksheets and samples for each section, such as letters to funding sources, interview forms, radio and newspaper announcements, information to include in the directory, and suggestions for volunteer training.

Older Volunteers, a Valuable Resource: A Guide for the Public and Private Sectors. Washington, DC: American Association of Retired Persons, 1986. 32p. Free.

This booklet highlights the essential points in effectively recruiting and using the services of older adult volunteers. Of particular importance is a section on how to say "no" when an applicant for a volunteer job is not suited to a position. Appendixes offer further resources including printed materials, technical assistance, and sources of volunteers. Order number D12025.

Retirees: A Profile of the 55-and-Over Market. Alexandria, VA: United Way of America, 1988. 65p. $10.

This highly readable overview has chapters on demographics, economics, geographic trends, life-styles and attitudes, employment and retirement trends, retirees as donors and volunteers, and corporate programs for retirees. It is an excellent resource for program planners. The background information will be valuable in volunteer recruitment and in preparing public-relations materials and presentations. The booklet was written for United Way agencies, but its usefulness is not limited to them. The appendixes contain statistical data, government agencies, model programs, and a bibliography. Order number USP0613.

Self-Help Guide to Volunteering. Denver, CO: Mile High United Way (The Volunteer Center, United Way Centennial Plaza, 2505 Eighteenth Street, Denver, CO 80211-3097), 1987. Free.

> This is a quick, effective self-assessment tool for use in making sound choices among the available volunteer opportunities. It explains the rewards that one might seek through a volunteer job. A set of questions helps potential volunteers decide which kinds of tasks they would most enjoy. There are tips to consider in deciding whether a particular type of organization will or will not be a desirable work environment. The brochure concludes with hints for making the most of a volunteer job.

"To Serve, Not To Be Served": A Guide for Older Volunteers. Washington, DC: American Association of Retired Persons, 1986. 24p. Free.

> This booklet takes its title from the motto upon which Dr. Ethel Percy Andrus founded AARP. It is a resource for the individual who is looking for a rewarding volunteer job. The publication explains the assets older adults brings to their volunteer work. In clear terms, it outlines methods of finding a suitable match between oneself and the unlimited opportunities for service. The booklet highlights the breadth of volunteer possibilities and a volunteer's responsibilities and rights. The appendixes give sources of further information and a generic list of volunteer possibilities in any locale, such as places of worship, courts, youth groups, and many more. Order number D12028.

Tobin, David, and Henry Ware. *The Barter Network Handbook: Building Community through Organized Trade.* Arlington, VA: VOLUNTEER– The National Center, 1983. 69p. $5.95.

> This handbook takes the reader from the initial question, "What is a barter network?" through the steps of creating and sustaining a network. Authors David Tobin and Henry Ware cite numerous examples of barter programs that serve such needs as transportation, legal services, home weatherization and maintenance, and auto repair. One chapter addresses barter and the Internal Revenue Service. The booklet includes a list of resources for further information and an index. Order number 103.

Vineyard, Sue. *Beyond Banquets, Plaques and Pins: Creative Ways To Recognize Volunteers & Staff!* Arlington, VA: VOLUNTEER–The National Center, 1981. 23p. $5.

> This noted volunteer-management expert offers a valuable resource to program directors and others who want thoughtful information on recognition. Vineyard explains why many traditional recognition events have lost their meaning. She then gives practical steps for expanding or changing recognition policies and establishing new ones. Checklists provide specific recognition ideas for volunteers of various circumstances; for example, seniors, church volunteers, and those who have low incomes. Other checklists have recognition ideas for different personality types. The publication includes a bibliography. Order number 98.

Volunteer Skills Portfolio, 2d ed. New York: Association of Junior Leagues (Jo Parks, The Association of Junior Leagues, Inc., 660 First Avenue, New York, NY 10016), 1987. 32p. $18.95.

> This is a workbook for individuals who plan to use their volunteer experience as a bridge to other pursuits such as career changes, higher volunteer-leadership positions, and further schooling. It is a guide to organizing and presenting volunteer experience, so it can garner the credit it deserves. Concrete examples of planning strategies, career goals, resumes, and interview techniques make it easy to follow. The *Portfolio* is designed for individual use and for groups.

Journal, Magazine, and Newspaper Articles

Bass, Sharon L. "Help Wanted, P/T, Immediate: Volunteers Please." *New York Times,* 3 July 1988.

> The article cites numerous examples of the needs for volunteers and the opportunities for challenging, meaningful service. With 72 percent of women age 25 to 54 in the work force, agencies are turning to students and older adults for help. Among the volunteer opportunities are firefighting, tutoring, family planning, assistance in community blood banks, interviewing in emergency health-service programs, staffing hotlines at family shelters, support and transportation for cancer patients, support for prison inmates, hospice work, and coaching Little League teams.

Although the persons interviewed represent programs in the New York City area, the examples of volunteer opportunities and the needs for volunteer service apply to any community in the United States.

Bond, John B., Jr. "Volunteerism and Life Satisfaction among Older Adults." *Canadian Counsellor* 16, 3 (1982): 168–172.

This study report concludes that 55- to 74-year-olds who donated their time and services through volunteer activities were more satisfied with their lives than their nonvolunteer counterparts. Education was identified as another contributor to life satisfaction. The instrument used to measure life satisfaction was the Life Satisfaction Index-A. Respondents were 373 men and women, both preretired and retired. The author conducted the study at the University of Manitoba where he is a faculty member. Program planners and researchers will find the article useful. A reference list, abstract, and tables are included.

Burden, Ordway P. "Volunteers: The Wave of the Future?" *The Police Chief* 55 (July 1988): 25–27.

The article gives examples of the growing participation of older adults as volunteers in local police departments. Their jobs range from staffing check-in systems for shut-ins to crime analysis and crime prevention. A study by the American Association of Retired Persons estimates that there are as many as 240,000 elder volunteers in law-enforcement agencies. A sidebar to the article describes a Palm Beach County, Florida, project in which physically handicapped persons enforce parking regulations. The feedback from law-enforcement officials indicates that initial resistance to volunteers often fades as they earn the respect of paid employees through outstanding performance.

Cantor, Carla. "Support Groups Fill Emotional Gaps." *New York Times*, 28 September 1986.

Self-help or mutual-aid groups now exist to help with practically any problem of daily life. For example, there are groups for suicide survivors, rape victims, children caring for elderly parents, post-mastectomy patients, tinnitus sufferers, and bereaved parents. Edward Madara, director of the New Jersey Self-Help Clearinghouse, comments, "Sometimes the most effective treatment is the knowledge you are not alone and help from others who have been there." The number of self-help groups nationwide may be as high as 500,000 with 15 million members. Psychologist Dr. John Kalafat speculates that the groups give people a perspective on their problems that they cannot obtain from paid professionals.

Drucker, Peter F. "What Business Can Learn from Nonprofits." *Harvard Business Review* 67 (July/August 1989): 88–93.

The renowned leader in business-management theory explains how nonprofit organizations have become more adept than businesses in motivating professional and volunteer staffs and achieving productivity. Drucker cites the following reasons: first, "The best nonprofits devote a great deal of thought to defining their organization's mission," second, "Many nonprofits now have what is still the exception in business—a functioning board," and third, the highly productive nonprofits give their volunteers challenging, responsible jobs, with high expectations for performance. "Volunteers must get far greater satisfaction from their accomplishments and make a greater contribution precisely because they do not get a paycheck." The article is a valuable review of key factors in successful management of nonprofit organizations. Program directors will be particularly interested in Drucker's remarks on volunteer accountability and satisfaction.

Duncombe, Sydney. "Volunteers in City Government: Getting More than Your Money's Worth." *National Civic Review* 75 (September/October 1986): 291–301.

This article reports findings from studies the author conducted in 1985 and 1986. The samples include volunteers and their supervisors. Volunteers most frequently worked as police auxiliaries, firefighters, recreation-program staff, library aides, assistants at senior citizen centers, file clerks/office workers, park-maintenance workers, and typists/secretaries. All respondents agreed that volunteers are a good supplement to paid staff and that volunteer contributions outweigh the costs. On the whole, supervisors were enthusiastic about working with volunteers. Often volunteers could give clients the individual attention that paid staff did not have the time to provide.

Ferris, James M. "Coprovision: Citizen Time and Money Donations in Public Service Provision." *Public Administration Review* 14 (July/August 1984): 324–333.

> This is a theoretical examination of "the voluntary actions of citizens, either through time or money donations, in the provision and production of publicly provided goods and services." Ferris defines coprovision as "the voluntary involvement of citizens in the *provision* of publicly provided goods and services or close substitutes." The information will be useful to researchers and policymakers who seek a framework for understanding how to measure the impact of volunteer involvement in government. Ferris is an economist with research interests in public finance and public-policy analysis. The article includes an abstract and extensive notes.

Gaioni, Kathleen, M.D. "Rx: Self-Help." *The New Physician* 37 (July/August 1988): 31–32.

> This is an enthusiastic endorsement of self-help groups by a physician who regularly recommends them to her patients as adjuncts to medical treatment. Gaioni says, "I have always wanted to provide a more durable support for my patients, especially for those coping with exceedingly stressful medical problems." She explains that groups use communication methods suited to the participants such as telephone conference lines and home computers as well as in-person meetings. The article includes specific references to self-help groups and, for further resources, the National Health Information Clearinghouse, (800) 336-4797.

Garbacz, Christopher, and Mark Thayer. "An Experiment in Valuing Senior Companion Program Services." *The Journal of Human Resources* 28 (Winter 1983): 147–153.

> In the face of rising questions about the effectiveness of publicly funded service programs, the authors describe an approach to placing a monetary value on these programs. For demonstration purposes, their experiment involved an analysis of the Senior Companion Program (SCP). A sample of SCP service recipients were asked what they would do if they had to purchase the services they got from SCP volunteers or had to make do with

less than their current level of service. The authors concluded that the SCP saves tax and individual dollars, and that some of its value cannot be measured in monetary terms. A reference list is included.

Goodman, Catherine Chase. "Helper Bank: A Reciprocal Services Program for Older Adults." *Social Work* 29 (July/August 1984): 397–398.

> The author describes the concept of the Helper Bank in which "a deposit represents a payment of labor, which provides entitlement for withdrawal, from the bank of similar services by the depositor." Typical services could be assistance in daily living such as transportation, cleaning, cooking, and emotional support through telephone conversations. Goodman discusses general administrative procedures for a hypothetical helper bank, but has no actual examples to cite in the article. This is a helpful source of ideas for volunteers and program planners who are considering this type of program.

Henderson, Carter. "Old Glory: America Comes of Age." *The Futurist* 22 (March/April 1988): 36–40.

> Economist Henderson makes a strong case for continued productivity among the nation's older citizens. His article provides an overview of the demographic, economic, and social implications of the aging of U.S. society. He documents how current retirement, employment, and taxation policies place a disproportionate burden on the middle-aged and the young. Henderson recommends that the increasingly well-educated older population remain productive. "America has the largest population of educated old people in the world, yet we have somehow failed to realize the miracle we have produced."

Hershberger, Barbara. "Living in the Freedom There Is." *Activities, Adaptation & Aging* 2 (Fall 1981): 51–58.

> This author challenges professional-service providers to focus attention not on the limitations of the elderly, but on their capabilities and potential. She decries the tendency to emphasize limitations, as with charts, for example, showing that older persons do not memorize illogical material as fast as younger persons; and tables showing loss of physical capacities starting in

young adulthood. Hershberger sums up her message, "People need to know what the real constraints are, but then turn and live in what freedom there is." This is an inspirational reminder that limitations and vitality can coexist. The article has notes and a bibliography.

Kahn, Ellie. "A Legend in Her Own Time." *Fifty Plus* 26 (July 1986): 34–37.

> This is a profile of 78-year-old Charlotte Pitts Dean, a heroine in her hometown of New London, New Hampshire. After she retired from teaching music, she and her husband designed second careers in community service, which she has continued since his death. At 4:00 A.M. each day Dean writes letters, up to 4,000 a year, to friends and to strangers "in need of love and sympathy and cheering up." Then she makes social calls by phone and in person. She arranges a daily program at the local nursing home and writes a weekly column for the community's newspaper, *The Argus-Champion*. Using Dean as a model, the article shows how individuals can design rewarding careers through self-directed volunteer work.

Kantrowitz, Barbara. "The New Volunteers." *Newsweek* 114 (10 July 1989): 36–66.

> This special report opens with a review of the current state of volunteerism in the United States. It notes that individuals between the ages of 65 to 74 give the most time to volunteer work, six hours a week. The second part profiles Barbara Bush who comments on social problems, "If it worries you, then you've got to do something about it." The third part of the report is a series of vignettes about "folks next door who just happen to be outstanding citizens." These are people of all ages who help others either through organized programs or in informal ways. The oldest is Frances Pauley, an 83-year-old social activist in Atlanta who has spent 60 years "showing poor people they count."

Kerschner, Helen K., and Frances F. Butler. "Productive Aging and Senior Volunteerism: Is the U.S. Experience Relevant?" *Ageing International* (December 1988): 15–19.

> The authors espouse a view of older persons as part of the solution to the problems of modern society. They offer, as options

for productivity, the Older American Volunteer Programs supported by the U.S. Government. These programs include the Retired Senior Volunteer Program (RSVP), the Foster Grandparent Program, and the Senior Companion Program. The list, Questions To Be Considered, is of use to volunteers, program coordinators, and policymakers in any community, although the target audience is program planners outside the United States. The article has notes and a list of resources.

Kouri, Mary K. "From Retirement to Re-Engagement: Young Elders Forge New Futures." *The Futurist* 28 (June 1984): 35–42.

> Kouri explains why thousands of young elders find that retirement is "banishment from important sources of meaning and satisfaction in their lives." Better education, better health, and greater financial independence equip this group for vigorous, productive lives. As an alternative to retirement, she proposes reengagement, "a new form of involvement in life . . . suited to the energies, interests, and capacities of one's present age." She describes practical steps for reengaging in new life-styles. The article will be of interest to individuals who seek guidance and encouragement in designing productive life activities.

Lunsford, Charlotte J. "Volunteering in 2001." *Vital Speeches of the Day* 54 (15 September 1988): 729–732.

> In her address to the National Volunteer Conference, Lunsford describes the changes that volunteer leaders, organizations, and volunteers themselves can anticipate in the near future. Regarding older volunteers, she predicts that nonprofit organizations will be competing with the job market for their involvement as employees. "If you doubt this trend, just visit your neighborhood MacDonald's." She cites retiree job banks as another competitor for the services of highly skilled retirees. She reminds her audience that volunteerism is still a source of compelling rewards, including opportunities for skill development, for seeing the results of one's work, and for networking.

McNurlen, Carolyn. "School Volunteers: Getting Involved Is Easy—and Rewarding." *Better Homes and Gardens* 64 (November 1986): 58.

This is a brief, comprehensive review of the many avenues for volunteerism in education. McNurlen shows that the possibilities extend well beyond bake sales. "Schools are hungry for . . . men and women, professionals and homemakers, managers and retirees, and just about everyone else who cares about the community." She lists a wide range of participation through which individual volunteers and organizations can help children and stretch education budgets. Volunteers and program directors will find this information useful.

Morrow-Howell, Nancy, DSW, and Martha N. Ozawa, Ph.D. "Helping Network: Seniors to Seniors." *The Gerontologist* 27 (February 1987): 17–20.

This article describes a program in St. Louis, Missouri, called the System To Assure Elderly Services (STAES). It is an innovative effort to connect needy elders with older volunteers who will provide supportive services such as telephone reassurance, companionship, shopping and transportation, and referrals. The authors describe the volunteer training and the functions of professional staff, of volunteer team leaders, and of field volunteers who work in the program. This model demonstrates the potential for efficiently and economically combining the efforts of paid and volunteer helpers for frail elders living in the community. The article contains an abstract and a reference list.

Nemy, Enid. "Age No Burden to Volunteers." *New York Times,* 2 October 1983.

This series of five volunteer profiles illustrates that the volunteer spirit can be vigorous well into life's eighth and ninth decades. The oldest volunteer is Hortense Hirsch, age 96; the "baby" of the group is 87. These five men and women work in a wide range of services including operating a hospital gift shop, fund-raising, political advocacy, sewing items for infants in hospitals, and programs for the blind. Hirsch takes a practical approach to her work, "I never know how I'm going to feel tomorrow. But I do what I can when I can." The article will be inspirational to volunteers and program planners.

Neugarten, Bernice L. "Age Groups in American Society and the Rise of the Young-Old." *Annals of the American Academy of Political and Social Sciences* 415 (September 1974): 187–198.

In this definitive article Neugarten introduced the idea that the age group 55 to 75 has characteristics that distinguish this stage of life from middle age and from old age. She coined the now-common term "young-old." They are "relatively healthy, relatively affluent, relatively free from traditional responsibilities of work and family, and . . . increasingly well educated and politically active." Neugarten points out that many 55- to 75-year-olds have at least one living parent. She says that the young-old are potential agents of social change and goodwill ambassadors among age groups. The article contains an abstract.

Pifer, Alan. "Put Out to Pasture Our Idea of Age 65." *New York Times,* 7 February 1984.

"Age 65 is obsolete," Pifer says. "It has become an anachronism as a basis of policy, as a result of improved health and startling increases in longevity for many Americans." He proposed that the "third quarter" of life (ages 50 to 75) be a period of major career change. These careers could involve paid work and/or volunteer service. "There must be a social expectation that people will remain productive throughout the third quarter of their lives and will be accepted by younger people as contributing, fully involved members of the community," Pifer concludes. The article will be of interest to elected officials and policymakers and to individuals who are planning their own life goals.

Stokes, Bruce. "Helping Ourselves." *The Futurist* 15 (August 1981): 44–51.

The author makes a strong case for self-help instead of dependence on "governments, corporations, and professional elites" for many of the things that people once did for themselves. He says that self-help results in stronger local communities and a better return on the public's money. For example, the Office of Neighborhood Self-Help Development estimates that every million dollars it invests in self-help projects is matched by $16 million from local sources. "Neighborhood friendships and local clubs . . . are the logical building blocks" for self-help activities. Program leaders, elected officials, and volunteers will find this article helpful.

Sweet, W. "Retired Scientists Provide Valuable Volunteer Work." *Physics Today* 37 (July 1984): 67–68.

This is a report on the American Association of Retired Persons' (AARP) effort to involve retired scientists in volunteer opportunities through its computerized Volunteer Talent Bank. The article describes successes and problems of the effort, which is still in the developmental stages. One recruitment problem is "Many retired scientists and engineers would resent any implication that they are unoccupied." Scientists work as volunteers in museums, public schools, universities, job fairs, and science fairs. The examples and resources will be helpful to individuals seeking challenging volunteer jobs and to program leaders.

Teltsch, Kathleen. "Program Allows Elderly To Barter for Services."
New York Times, 23 February 1987.

The Service Credit Volunteer System described here is one of a growing number of service banks. "It operates much like a blood bank. Participants who perform chores receive service credits that are banked and can be tapped in time of need." Friends and family can earn credits and transfer them to an individual's account. A computer handles the tasks of bookkeeping and matching requests with services; this keeps the staff costs down. The author notes the rising interest of government agencies and foundations in service banks. She adds, "They are regarded approvingly by some gerontologists as an imaginative way to use the resources of a growing number of older Americans."

Chapter 6

Electronic Media, Films, and Videos

This is a diverse collection of resources for use in all aspects of volunteerism. There are selections for prospective and current volunteers, professional staff, for volunteer leaders, and for researchers. The videotapes on specific programs will be useful to individuals in choosing volunteer jobs and in volunteer recruitment as well. Program managers will find training aids for volunteers and professional staff. For nonprofit organizations, the administration and communication tools will be helpful. For researchers and students, the databases are keys to a wealth of information.

Electronic Media

AgeLine Database
National Gerontology Resource Center
American Association of Retired Persons (AARP)
1909 K Street, NW
Washington, DC 20049
(202) 728-4880

> AgeLine provides citations from journal articles, books, government documents, reports, chapters, dissertations, and conference papers. The database includes materials published since 1978 with a few exceptions. Citations include literature from the areas of aging and economics, family relationships, demographics, political involvement, and health-care services. Updates are

bimonthly. The AgeLine vendor is Bibliographic Retrieval Services (BRS), (800) 345-4277; in New York, (518) 783-1161. Access is available through many libraries and direct subscription to BRS.

Foundation Directory Database
The Foundation Center
79 Fifth Avenue
New York, NY 10003
(212) 620-4230

> The Foundation Directory contains information on the program interests of charitable foundations, their officers and trustees, publications, application guidelines, and grants awarded. The database is available on-line through DIALOG Information Services, (800) 334-2564. Specify the file number (26) as well as the name in making inquiries. Contact DIALOG for guidance in accessing the database. Call the Foundation Center for more information on the data-base contents.

Grants Index Database
The Foundation Center
79 Fifth Avenue
New York, NY 10003
(212) 620-4230

> The Grants Index Database offers quick access to information on grants available, grant recipients, and sources of grant funds such as foundations, governmental agencies, and others. Application guidelines and deadlines are included. Cross-indexing makes it possible to scan grants for specific project ideas or population groups. The Grants Index Database is available on-line through DIALOG Information Services, (800) 334-2564. Specify the file number (27) as well as the name in making inquiries. Contact DIALOG for guidance in accessing the database. Call the Foundation Center for more information on the data-base contents.

Private Sector Initiatives (PSI) Network
United Way of America
Stephen L. Rose, Director, Information Services
701 North Fairfax Street
Alexandria, VA 22314-2045
(703) 683-7883

VOLUNTEER–The National Center
Kay Drake, Director, Information Services
1111 North Nineteenth Street, Suite 500
Arlington, VA 22209
(703) 276-0542

> The PSI Network provides detailed information on private-sector-based projects in the United States that have demonstrated success in their communities. Project reports may be accessed by category, for example, "Volunteerism." The network is a tool for program planning, research, information sharing, and keeping abreast of developments. Cross-indexing makes it readily accessible. Project reports are fairly detailed and include contact information. Reports can be printed on IBM PC or PS/2 compatible microcomputers. Nonsubscribers may purchase hard copies of reports. The PSI Network is a joint project of four organizations: ACTION–The Federal Domestic Volunteer Agency, VOLUNTEER–The National Center, the White House Office of National Service, and United Way of America.

Resource Match Software and User's Guide
VOLUNTEER–The National Center
1111 North Nineteenth Street, Suite 500
Arlington, VA 22209
(703) 276-0542

> This administration tool stores resource data such as volunteers, their skills, in-kind donations, workshops, and other resources. It matches resources with needs, tracks activity, and generates reports and letters. The software is useful in operating skillsbanks. The program is menu driven and can be customized to handle a wide range of information. Purchasers receive six months of telephone and mail technical assistance. The IBM-Compatible (requires hard disk and 512K memory) package costs $779, order number 172. The Apple IIe version is $295, order number 173. A preview booklet is available; specify IBM or Apple version. Order number 174, $10.

VOLNET Electronic Communications Network
VOLUNTEER–The National Center
1111 North Nineteenth Street, Suite 500
Arlington, VA 22209
(703) 276-0542

VOLNET offers four features. (1) *VOLNET News Magazine,* biweekly, carries legislative and research updates, resources, computer-usage tips, and program notes. (2) Biweekly Bulletin Boards announce conferences, reports, and developments in volunteerism. (3) Personal Electronic Mailboxes enable users to correspond with other organizations and individuals. (4) Special Networks and Services allow members to establish their own networks. VOLUNTEER–The National Center's staff provide technical assistance. Required equipment is a computer, modem, and communications software. VOLNET is a VOLUNTEER membership benefit; nonmembers pay $50 a year. All Personal Electronic Mailbox subscribers pay a small extra charge.

Films and Videos

The Best of You . . . the Best of Me

Type:	Videocassette, BETA, VHS, 3/4″ U-Matic
Length:	27 min.
Date:	1986
Cost:	Purchase $100; rental $50 for 2 days, applicable toward purchase, plus $4 for postage and insurance
Source:	Generations Together–BOYBOM University of Pittsburgh 811 William Pitt Union Pittsburgh, PA 15260

The film highlights six outstanding intergenerational programs in Pennsylvania. It is useful in raising awareness about the range of intergenerational program possibilities, in providing information for program development, and in demonstrating the human impact of intergenerational contacts. A program-implementation manual accompanies the order.

Hometown USA

Type:	Videocassette, 3/4″, VHS
Length:	10 min.
Date:	Not listed
Cost:	For loan only, no cost
Source:	AARP A/V Programs Resource Promotion Section/BV 1909 K Street, NW Washington, DC 20049

This videotape offers an overview of volunteer opportunities in the American Association of Retired Persons' (AARP) Program and Field Services Division. Volunteers are involved in health issues, respite for older care givers, tax assistance, citizen representation, criminal-justice services, emotional support for widows and widowers, reminiscence, and intergenerational exchanges.

How Am I Going To Recruit Them?
Let It Shine: Motivating and Training Volunteers
Type: Videocassette, VHS
Length: Information not available
Cost: Tape $38 (both modules on one tape), written materials $2.50 for one copy ($13 for ten copies)
Source: Project VOTE!
           1424 Sixteenth Street, NW, Suite 101
           Washington, DC 20035
           (202) 328-1500

This training package, all on one tape, teaches five keys to volunteer motivation through the "Tell/Show/Do" training cycle. The material is applicable to all types of volunteers. As a teaching example, *Let It Shine* shows how to prepare an organizer to run a motivation and training session for voter-registration volunteers. *How Am I Going To Recruit Them?* demonstrates the key elements of a volunteer-recruitment pitch and follow-up calls to make sure volunteers show up. Written materials for the package include tips and sample pitches for different situations, guidelines on finding volunteer leads, and problem-solving techniques for recruitment situations.

In Their Shoes
Type: Videocassette, VHS
Length: 15 min.
Date: 1981
Cost: Loan only, no cost
Source: Peace Corps
           Public Affairs
           Audiovisual Department
           Washington, DC 20526
           (800) 424-8580

This film highlights the service of older Peace Corps volunteers serving in the Caribbean and Central America. Peace Corps headquarters will give information for borrowing the tape from one of its regional offices.

Let It Begin Here

Type:	Videocassette, VHS
Length:	37 min.
Date:	1988
Cost:	For loan only, no cost
Source:	Peace Corps
	Public Affairs
	Audiovisual Department
	Washington, DC 20526
	(800) 424-8580

This tape features Peace Corps volunteers in Morocco, Mali, and Honduras. It gives examples of Peace Corps work and glimpses of the settings in which volunteers serve. Peace Corps headquarters will provide information on borrowing the tape from one of its regional offices.

Mine Forever

Type:	Videocassette, 3/4", VHS
Length:	18 min.
Date:	Not listed
Cost:	For loan only, no cost
Source:	AARP A/V Programs
	Resource Promotion Section/BV
	1909 K Street, NW
	Washington, DC 20049

This film title is borrowed from a statement by Dr. Ethel Percy Andrus, founder of the American Association of Retired Persons (AARP): "What I spent is gone, what I kept is lost, but what I gave away is mine forever." It tells the story of AARP's 250,000 volunteers. They serve as community leaders, advocates, counselors, teachers and trainers, workers, resources, and often, simply as friends to millions of other older adults. Individual volunteers tell how their activities enrich their lives.

Share It with the Children: A Preschool Curriculum on Aging
Type: Videocassette, VHS
Length: 17 min.
Date: 1988
Cost: Purchase $75, plus $4 postage and handling; rental $25, plus
           $4 postage and handling
Source: Generations Together—SIWTC
           University of Pittsburgh
           811 William Pitt Union
           Pittsburgh, PA 15260

> This tape shows model intergenerational activities in three child-
> care centers. Its intended audience is child-development agencies
> and older-adult programs that are interested in starting inter-
> generational activities. *Share It with the Children* is part of a
> preschool curriculum on aging. In its entirety, the curriculum
> presents 45 tested and evaluated preschool activities. The how-to
> section explains how to recruit and train older adult volunteers
> and how to maintain and evaluate intergenerational preschool
> programs.

To Care: America's Voluntary Spirit
Type: 16mm color film; videocassette, 3/4″, VHS, BETA
Length: 25 min.
Date: 1983
Cost: Film purchase $450 for nonmembers, $275 for members of Inde-
           pendent Sector; videocassette purchase $225 for nonmembers,
           $169 for members of Independent Sector; film or videocassette
           rental $50
Source: Films Incorporated
           733 Green Bay Road
           Wilmette, IL 60091
           (800) 323-4222, Education Division, ext. 338

> This tape was commissioned by Independent Sector to (1) show
> the extent and diversity of volunteerism in the United States; (2)
> clarify the roles of foundations, corporate giving programs, and
> voluntary organizations; and (3) encourage volunteerism among
> nonvolunteers. Independent Sector is a nonprofit organization
> dedicated to preserving and enhancing this country's tradition of
> giving, volunteering, and not-for-profit initiative. A free guide

for using *To Care* is available from Independent Sector, 1828 L Street, NW, Washington, DC 20036; (202) 223-8100.

The Toughest Job You'll Ever Love

Type:	Videocassette, VHS
Length:	26 min.
Date:	1979
Cost:	For loan only, no cost
Source:	Peace Corps
	Public Affairs
	Audiovisual Department
	Washington, DC 20526
	(800) 424-8580

This tape is an introduction to service in the Peace Corps. It features the work of a bridge builder in Nepal, a home economist in Colombia, and a health specialist in Niger. Peace Corps headquarters will give information for borrowing the tape from one of its regional offices.

Index

AA (Alcoholics Anonymous), 84
AARP (American Association of Retired
Persons), 12, 85–90
*AARP Publications & A/V Programs: The
Complete Collection,* 90, 164
*Abundance of Life: Human Development
Policies for an Aging Society,* 150
ACE (Active Corps Executives), 119
Acknowledgment, of volunteers, 77–79, 169
ACS (American Cancer Society), 90
"Action Alerts," 101
Active Corps Executives, 119
ADRDA (Alzheimer's Disease and Related
Disorders Association, Inc.), 84–85, 107
"Age Groups in American Society and the
Rise of the Young-Old," 176–177
"Age No Burden to Volunteers," 176
*Age Wave: The Challenges and
Opportunities of an Aging America,* 148
AgeLine Database, 179–180
Aging, 45, 161, 185
Agricultural museums, 93, 158–159
AHS (American Hiking Society) Volunteer
Vacations, 91–92
AIDS services, 54, 132
Al-Anon Family Groups, 83–84
Alcoholics Anonymous, 84
Alcoholism, organizations for, 46, 83–84
ALHFAM (Association for Living Historical
Farms and Agricultural Museums, Inc.),
93
All the World, 117
"All Things Considered," 112
Alzheimer's disease, organizations for, 46,
54, 84–85, 107
Alzheimer's Disease and Related Disorders
Association, Inc., 84–85, 107
American Association for International
Aging, 164–165

American Association of Retired Persons, 12,
85–90
American Cancer Society, 90
American Heart Association, 90–91
"The American Heart Association Diet," 91
American Hiking Society Volunteer
Vacations, 91–92
American Red Cross, 92
American Society of Directors of Volunteer
Services of the American Hospital
Association, 128–129
*America's Voluntary Spirit: A Book of
Readings,* 131–132, 151
Anderson, Jay, 156
Andrus, Ethel Percy, 85, 184
Anthes, Earl, 145
Aramony, William, 135, 146
Arbor Day, 105
ARC (American Red Cross), 92
ASDVS (American Society of Directors of
Volunteer Services of the American
Hospital Association), 128–129
"Assessment of the Department of Volunteer
Services in a Health Care Institution,"
128
Association for Living Historical Farms and
Agricultural Museums, Inc., 93
Association for Volunteer Administration, 129
Assumptions about older volunteers, 69–70
*Attitudes of Americans over 45 Years of Age
on Volunteerism,* 165
AVA (Association for Volunteer
Administration), 129

Banks
blood, 46, 92
service, 12, 32, 173, 178
skills, 99, 153
talent, 51, 86

187